■ DRUGS
The Straight Facts

Alzheimer's Disease and Memory Drugs

DRUGS The Straight Facts

■ DRUGS
The Straight Facts

Alzheimer's Disease and Memory Drugs

Cynthia Borda

Consulting Editor
David J. Triggle
University Professor
School of Pharmacy and Pharmaceutical Sciences
State University of New York at Buffalo

CHELSEA HOUSE
PUBLISHERS
An imprint of Infobase Publishing

Alzheimer's Disease and Memory Drugs

Chelsea House
An imprint of Infobase Publishing
132 West 31st Street
New York NY 10001

Library of Congress Cataloging-in-Publication Data

Borda, Cynthia
    Alzheimer's disease and memory drugs / Cynthia Borda.
        p. cm.—(Drugs, the straight facts)
    ISBN 0-7910-8555-4
    1. Alzheimer's disease—Juvenile literature. 2. Alzheimer's disease—Treatment—Juvenile literature. 3. Alzheimer's disease—Chemotherapy—Juvenile literature. I. Title. II. Series.
    RC523.3.B67 2006
    616.8'31061—dc22   2005032189

Chelsea House books are available at special discounts when purchased in bulk quantities for businesses, associations, institutions, or sales promotions. Please call our Special Sales Department in New York at (212) 967-8800 or (800) 322-8755.

You can find Chelsea House on the World Wide Web at http://www.chelseahouse.com

Text and cover design by Terry Mallon

Printed in the United States of America

Bang 21C 10 9 8 7 6 5 4 3 2 1

This book is printed on acid-free paper.

All links and web addresses were checked and verified to be correct at the time of publication. Because of the dynamic nature of the web, some addresses and links may have changed since publication and may no longer be valid.

Table of Contents

The Use and Abuse of Drugs

The issues associated with drug use and abuse in contemporary society are vexing subjects, fraught with political agendas and ideals that often obscure essential information that teens need to know to have intelligent discussions about how to best deal with the problems associated with drug use and abuse. *Drugs: The Straight Facts* aims to provide this essential information through straightforward explanations of how an individual drug or group of drugs works in both therapeutic and non-therapeutic conditions; with historical information about the use and abuse of specific drugs; with discussion of drug policies in the United States; and with an ample list of further reading.

From the start, the series uses the word *"drug"* to describe psychoactive substances that are used for medicinal or non-medicinal purposes. Included in this broad category are substances that are legal or illegal. It is worth noting that humans have used many of these substances for hundreds, if not thousands of years. For example, traces of marijuana and cocaine have been found in Egyptian mummies; the use of peyote and Amanita fungi has long been a component of religious ceremonies worldwide; and alcohol production and consumption have been an integral part of many human cultures' social and religious ceremonies. One can speculate about why early human societies chose to use such drugs. Perhaps, anything that could provide relief from the harshness of life—anything that could make the poor conditions and fatigue associated with hard work easier to bear—was considered a welcome tonic. Life was likely to be, according to the seventeenth century English philosopher Thomas Hobbes, *"poor, nasty, brutish and short."* One can also speculate about modern human societies' continued use and abuse of drugs. Whatever the reasons, the consequences of sustained drug use are not insignificant—addiction, overdose, incarceration, and drug wars—and must be dealt with by an informed citizenry.

The problem that faces our society today is how to break the connection between our demand for drugs and the willingness of largely outside countries to supply this highly profitable trade. This is the same problem we have faced since narcotics and cocaine were outlawed by the Harrison Narcotic Act of 1914, and we have yet to defeat it despite current expenditures of approximately $20 billion per year on "the war on drugs." The first step in meeting any challenge is always an intelligent and informed citizenry. The purpose of this series is to educate our readers so that they can make informed decisions about issues related to drugs and drug abuse.

SUGGESTED ADDITIONAL READING

David T. Courtwright, *Forces of Habit. Drugs and the Making of the Modern World.* Cambridge, Mass.: Harvard University Press, 2001. David Courtwright is Professor of History at the University of North Florida.

Richard Davenport-Hines, *The Pursuit of Oblivion. A Global History of Narcotics.* New York: Norton, 2002. The author is a professional historian and a member of the Royal Historical Society.

Aldous Huxley, *Brave New World.* New York: Harper & Row, 1932. Huxley's book, written in 1932, paints a picture of a cloned society devoted only to the pursuit of happiness.

David J. Triggle, Ph.D.
University Professor
School of Pharmacy and Pharmaceutical Sciences
State University of New York at Buffalo

1

Defining Alzheimer's Disease

Did you ever briefly forget your friend's name or have trouble recalling the name of a song on the radio? Many of us joke that it is an "early form of Alzheimer's." However, if you are younger than 60, the likelihood that you have Alzheimer's disease (AD) is slim. The memory loss that most people experience can be attributed to many different reasons, such as lack of sleep, too much on their mind, anxiety, or depression. This memory loss tends to be brief, occasional, and has little impact on daily life.

Memory loss that occurs more frequently and that begins to impact a person's life, however, is usually a type of dementia. Dementias are usually irreversible and not curable. Dementia primarily affects the elderly and can have many origins. AD is the most common form of dementia, occurring about 65% of the time. However, it is also important to rule out other forms of dementia (**differential diagnosis**). Table 1.1 lists potential causes of dementia (sometimes referred to as "senility"). Many of these causes, such as those listed under infections, metabolic disorders, medications, and vitamin deficiencies, can be treated and the dementia abates.

Since there are many possible reasons for dementia-like attributes, it is important to see a neurologist. A **neurologist** is a medical doctor who specializes in the brain and the disorders that affect the brain. Neurologists often specialize in a particular brain disorder. For instance, one neurologist may treat primarily patients who have had a stroke (temporary or permanent loss of some body functioning),

(continued on page 12)

Table 1.1 Potential causes of dementia.

Neurologic disorders	Stroke, Transient ischemic attack, Biswanger's disease, Alzheimer's disease, Lewy body dementia, Parkinson's disease, Huntington's disease, Pick's disease, Creutzfeldt-Jakob disease
Infections	Encephalitis, Meningitis
Metabolic disorders	Thyroid, Pancreatic, Adrenal
Cardiovascular disorders	Vascular occlusion
Medications	• Anticholinergics—blocks action of acetylcholine, a nerve transmitter • Sedative/hypnotic—sleeping pills • Antihypertensives—blood pressure medicine
Toxins	Heavy metals
Mental illness	Schizophrenia, Depression, Substance abuse
Vitamin deficiencies	B_{12}, Folate
Intracranial causes	Tumors, Subdural hematoma, Hydrocephalus, Abcesses

Shirley KL, Jann MW. Dementia. Pharmacotherapy Self-Assessment Program Fourth Ed. ACCP. Kansas City, MO 64111

NEURONS: THE GREAT COMMUNICATORS

There are billions of **neurons** within our brains. Collectively, neurons make up the nervous system, which continually signals the brain and tells it what to do. The central nervous system coordinates all the reactions and actions of the body, such as hearing, smelling, seeing, running, sleeping, blinking, breathing, and the beating of the heart.

Each neuron has a job to do and must be a team player. A neuron has a body that contains the nucleus, which controls all the cell's activities. The axon is an extension from the cell body and transmits messages to other neurons. These axons are capable of transmitting messages over distances of up to five feet. Finally, dendrites are cell extensions responsible for receiving messages from other neurons. The neurons are surrounded by **glial cells**, which protect and nourish them (Figure A). In order for neurons to survive they must work together to constantly communicate, generate their own energy, and clean and repair themselves.

Communication—When a neuron receives a message (an electrical impulse) through its dendrites, it sends the message along the axon. At the end of the axon, the electrical impulse triggers the release of **neurotransmitters** or chemical messengers. These neurotransmitters travel across a small gap called a **synapse** to another neuron's dendrite. Every neurotransmitter has its own specific receptors on the dendrite, which signal the neuron. Some signals will inhibit a process, and others stimulate a process. At any point in time, there are millions of neurons firing signals within the brain. If the neurons become disconnected (the signal is stopped), they do not survive.

Energy—Neurons need energy to keep working. Energy is provided by glucose, a type of sugar, which is obtained from eating food. Metabolism is another source of energy. **Metabolism** is a process that creates energy by breaking down chemicals and nutrients. In addition, metabolism needs oxygen, provided

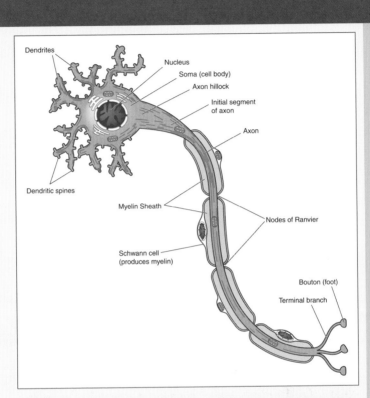

Figure A *A neuron has a body that contains the nucleus, which controls all the cell's activities. The axon is an extension from the cell body and transmits messages to other neurons. Dendrites are cell extensions responsible for receiving messages from other neurons.*

by the circulating blood. Without both oxygen and glucose, the neurons will die.

Repair—Another function that neurons need is self-maintenance. The neurons we are born with are often stay with us until death. This is because neurons are constantly repairing themselves, remodeling themselves, and doing cell clean up. If these processes slow down or stop, the neurons can no longer function.

(continued from page 8)

while other neurologists may treat primarily Alzheimer's patients. Therefore, choosing an appropriate neurologist is one of the first steps in determining the correct diagnosis.

The neurologist will then assist in determining if a patient has a form of dementia. If it is concluded that it is dementia, the neurologist will further attempt to determine the likely cause. For specific information on various tests for dementia and AD, please refer to Chapter 4.

HISTORY OF ALZHEIMER'S DISEASE

A German neuropathologist and psychiatrist named Alois Alzheimer (see "Alois Alzheimer" box) studied a 51-year-old female patient with severe dementia. The woman started experiencing symptoms five years earlier, such as memory loss and trouble reading and writing. She rapidly declined to hallucinations and was unable to take care of herself.

ALOIS ALZHEIMER

Dr. Alois Alzheimer was born on June 14, 1864, in Bavaria. He attended the universities of Aschaffenburg, Tübingen, Berlin, and Würzburg, where he received a medical degree in 1887. The following year, Alzheimer joined the medical staff at the city mental asylum in Frankfurt, Germany. While he first began his career in psychiatry, Alzheimer quickly devoted himself to his great interest of **neuropathology**, the study of the causes, nature, and effects of brain diseases.

In 1903, he moved to the university psychiatric clinic in Munich. He recorded his findings on his first AD patient in 1907. For the next ten years, he studied patients with **syphilis**, **Huntington's disease**, **epilepsy**, and a **pseudosclerosis** of the brain now known as Wilson's disease. Alois Alzheimer died on December 19, 1915, at the age of 51, due to cardiac failure following endocarditis, inflammation of the membrane that lines the heart and forms part of the heart valves.

When Dr. Alzheimer's patient died, he was able to study her brain at autopsy.

Alzheimer noted that the **cerebral cortex**, the outer layer of the brain responsible for numerous functions such as movement, perception, memory, and speaking, was thinner than normal and had severe atrophy. He also noted two other abnormalities. The first was "senile plaque" (now known as **neuritic plaque**) that had earlier been seen in the brains of the elderly. Second, there were **neurofibrillary tangles** within the cortex that had not been previously described. These hallmarks for which Alzheimer coined the term *presenile dementia*, are now known as Alzheimer's disease (Figure 1.1). Neuritic plaques and neurofibrillary tangles will be discussed in more detail in Chapter 3. Interestingly, to this day, the only way to definitively know that a person has AD is at autopsy.

WHO GETS ALZHEIMER'S DISEASE

It is estimated that over 4 million Americans have Alzheimer's disease. It is also estimated that by the year 2050, the number could increase to 14 million. One out of every ten persons 65 years of age and older develops AD, although some develop it in their 40s and 50s. Alzheimer's affects approximately 20% of people between the ages of 75 and 84. The percentage of AD increases to almost 50% in Americans 85 years and older.

The clinical course of the disease is between 2 years and 20 years from the onset of symptoms until death, with an average of about 8 years. There are about 360,000 new cases of Alzheimer's diagnosed every year and about 100,000 deaths each year from AD.[1, 2]

Alzheimer's disease affects people from all walks of life. The death of President Ronald Reagan from complications of AD has re-ignited an interest in finding a cure for the disease. Other famous people with Alzheimer's include actors Charles Bronson, Rita Hayworth, Charlton Heston, Jack Lord, and James Doohan; sports stars Sugar Ray Robinson, Joe

Figure 1.1 Alois Alzheimer (pictured here) is the German neurologist who is credited with discovering Alzheimer's disease.

Adcock, Bill Quackenbush, and Tom Fears; E.B. White, the author of the children's classic *Charlotte's Web*, and Barry Goldwater, former senator of Arizona.

THE IMPACT OF ALZHEIMER'S

Alzheimer's disease not only affects the patients but also the patient's family. Almost one out of three households in the

Figure 1.2 Almost one out of three households in the United States is affected by Alzheimer's disease. An estimated 75% of Alzheimer's patients receive home care.

United States is affected by AD. A little over half of the care provided to AD patients is at home; some estimates place the care at home closer to 75% (Figure 1.2). The combination of healthcare expenses and the loss of income of both the patient and the caregiver is approaching $100 billion nationwide. The average cost per patient from the onset of symptoms until death is about $174,000.

Over half of the nursing home residents in the United States have AD or some other form of dementia. The annual cost of caring for an AD patient ranges from $18,400 for mild symptoms to $36,132 for those with advanced symptoms. In addition, the average cost of nursing home care is almost $58,000 a year. Medicare and most health insurance plans do not cover the care of an AD patient since it is considered "custodial care."[1, 2]

Caregivers are a subset of the Alzheimer's picture that is often overlooked. Stress and depression are reported frequently among caregivers: depression affects approximately 50% of caregivers, with stress occurring in at least 80%. Not surprisingly, the emotional, financial, and sometimes physical burden of witnessing a loved one decline mentally and physically is often overwhelming.

SUPPORT AND HOPE

There are several organizations dedicated to educating patients, families, and caregivers about Alzheimer's, providing helpful insights into where to go for help and support. These organizations are listed in the Resources section of this book.

Researchers have been studying the AD brain, with all its complexities, since Alois Alzheimer presented his patient in 1907. Science is now closer to finding some answers about what may cause AD, and therefore gaining momentum on what may prevent or treat the disease.

2

An Overview of Brain Function

The changes that occur in the brain in Alzheimer's disease provide some background to the medications used in this disease. It is important to keep in mind that there is currently no definitive explanation as to why this disease process begins. First, it is essential to have some knowledge of the functions of the brain to understand Alzheimer's and how the medications are developed and utilized.

THE BRAIN

The human brain is a complex organ that allows us to think, move, feel, see, hear, taste, and smell. It controls our body, receives information, analyzes information, and stores information (our memories). The brain produces electrical signals, which, together with chemical reactions, let the parts of the body communicate. Nerves send these signals throughout the body.

The average human brain weighs about three pounds (1300–1400 grams). As a comparison, a half-gallon of water weighs about four pounds. The brain consists of gray matter (40%) and white matter (60%) contained within the skull. Brain cells include neurons and glial cells. Although the brain is only 2% of the body's weight, it uses 20% of the oxygen supply and gets 20% of the blood flow. If brain cells do not get oxygen for 3 to 5 minutes, they begin to die.

The brain and spinal cord make up the central nervous system (CNS). The brain is connected to the spinal cord, which runs from the neck to the hip area. The spinal cord carries nerve messages between the brain and the body. The cells of the nervous system are quite fragile and need extensive protection from being crushed, infected by disease organisms, and other harm. The brain and spinal cord are covered by a tough, translucent membrane called the dura matter. Cerebrospinal fluid (CSF) is a clear, watery liquid that surrounds the brain and spinal cord and is also found throughout the ventricles (brain cavities and tunnels). CSF cushions the brain and spinal cord from jolts.

The cranium (the top of the skull) surrounds and protects the brain. The spinal cord is surrounded by vertebrae (hollow spinal bones) and also some muscles serve to pad and support

THE BLOOD BRAIN BARRIER

In the early 1900s, researchers discovered that when blue dye was injected into the bloodstream of an animal, all of the tissues and organs of the body turned blue except for the brain and spinal cord. This indicated that there was a special barrier that prevented some substances from entering the central nervous system through the bloodstream. This barrier is now called the blood brain barrier (BBB). The basic attributes of the BBB are as follows:

1. Large molecules do not pass through the BBB easily.

2. Lipid (fat) soluble molecules, such as barbiturate drugs, rapidly cross the BBB into the brain. However, low lipid soluble molecules do not.

3. Molecules that have a high electrical charge to them are slowed as they pass through the BBB.

The BBB is semi-permeable, which means it allows some materials to pass through it but prevents others from doing so. The smallest blood vessels in the body are called capillaries and are lined with endothelial cells. Endothelial tissue has small spaces between each individual cell so the spine. More subtly, the blood-brain barrier protects the brain from chemical intrusion from the rest of the body. Blood flowing into the brain is filtered so that many harmful chemicals cannot enter the brain.

The brain has three main parts, the cerebrum, the cerebellum, and the brain stem (Figure 2.1). The brain is divided into regions that control specific functions.

THE CEREBRUM

The cerebrum is the largest part of the brain and is responsible for all voluntary (conscious) activities of the body. It is the

substances can move readily between the inside and the outside of the vessel. In the brain, however, the endothelial cells fit tightly together and substances cannot pass out of the bloodstream.

The functions of the BBB are to protect the brain from "foreign substances" in the blood that may injure the brain and to protect it from the hormones and neurotransmitters in the rest of the body. The BBB also maintains a constant environment for the brain.

Various conditions can cause a breakdown in the function of the BBB. These conditions are as follows:

- Hypertension (high blood pressure).
- Incomplete development of the BBB at birth.
- High concentrations of certain substances in the blood.
- Exposure to microwaves.
- Exposure to radiation.
- Infection.
- Trauma or injury to the brain.

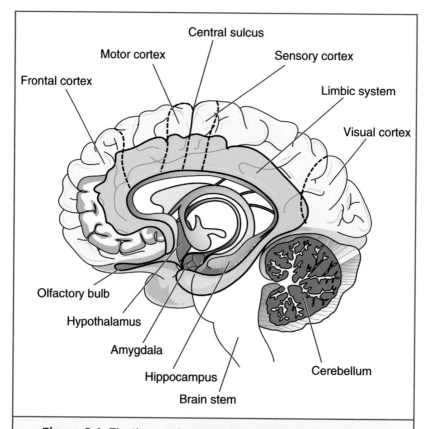

Central sulcus

Motor cortex

Sensory cortex

Frontal cortex

Limbic system

Visual cortex

Olfactory bulb

Hypothalamus

Amygdala

Hippocampus

Cerebellum

Brain stem

Figure 2.1 The three main areas of the brain are the cerebrum, the cerebellum, and the brain stem. Each region performs specific functions. The cerebrum, which includes the cerebral cortex, controls conscious activities, the cerebellum coordinates muscle movements, and the brain stem is responsible for vital body processes.

area of intelligence, learning, and judgment. The cerebrum is the functional area of language, personality, vision, memory, emotion, problem solving, initiative, inhibition, sense of smell, generalized and mass movements, motor skills, physical reaction, and libido (sexual urges).

The cerebrum is divided into two hemispheres, the left hemisphere and the right hemisphere (Figure 2.2). These

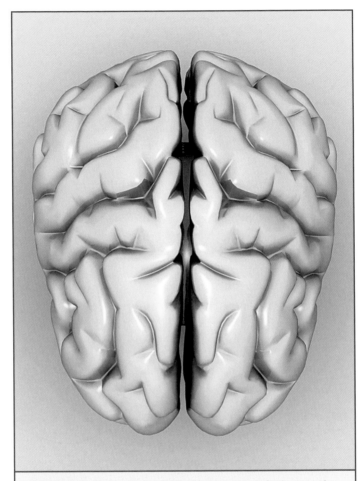

Figure 2.2 The brain is divided into two hemispheres—the right hemisphere and the left. The right hemisphere controls the left side of the body and creative ability. The left side of the brain controls the right side of the body is responsible for analytical ability.

hemispheres communicate with each other by way of a bundle of neurons called a tract. This tract is within an area of the brain called the corpus callosum. Each hemisphere is divided into four lobes. These lobes are called the frontal, parietal, temporal, and occipital lobes; each lobe has certain functions.

Frontal Lobe

Behavior

Abstract thought processes

Problem solving

Attention

Creative thought

Some emotions

Intellect

Reflection

Judgment

Initiative

Inhibition

Coordination of movements

Generalized and mass movements

Some eye movements

Sense of smell

Muscle movements

Skilled movements

Some motor skills

Physical reactions

Libido (sexual urges)

Occipital Lobe

Vision

Reading

Parietal Lobe

Sense of touch

Appreciation of form through touch

Response to internal stimuli

Sensory combination and comprehension

Some language and reading functions

Some visual functions

Temporal Lobe

    Auditory memories
    Some hearing functions
    Visual memories
    Some vision pathways
    Other memory
    Music
    Fear
    Some language
    Some speech functions
    Some behavior and emotions
    Sense of identity

Researchers have discovered that each side of the brain (hemisphere) is associated with different abilities.

Right Hemisphere (the creative hemisphere)

    Controls the left side of the body
    Creativity and artistic ability

Left Hemisphere (the analytical hemisphere)

    Controls the right side of the body
    Produce and understand language
    Analytical and mathematical ability

Finally, the cerebrum consists of two types of surfaces, an outer and an inner surface. The outer surface is called the cerebral cortex and consists of layers of neurons without myelin (fatty insulation). These layers appear to be gray in color and are therefore referred to as "gray matter." The inner surface is called the cerebral medulla, which consists of layers of myelinated neurons. The myelin is white and therefore these inner layers are referred to as "white matter."

THE CEREBELLUM

The cerebellum is the second largest part of the brain and sits at the back of the skull. Its major function is to coordinate all muscle movements. Therefore, it controls balance and posture, and the cardiac, respiratory, and vasomotor centers. The actions of the cerebellum are involuntary, so learning new physical skills can be very difficult for someone who has a natural lack of coordination.

THE BRAIN STEM

The brain stem connects the brain to the spinal cord. It serves as the motor and sensory pathway to the body and face, along with controlling such vital body processes as cardiac (heart), respiratory (lungs), and vasomotor functions (relating to the nerves or muscles that cause the blood vessels to constrict or dilate). The brain stem is made up of four parts: the medulla oblongata, pons, midbrain, and diencephalon.

The medulla oblongata (or medulla) is the lowest part of the brain stem. It is responsible for conducting impulses between the spinal cord and the brain. The medulla is the control center for involuntary movements such as breathing, blood pressure, blinking, heart rate, digestion, swallowing, and coughing. Also, within the medulla is a group of cells called the reticular activating system (RAS), which assist the brain in staying alert. An example would be waking up to an alarm clock.

The pons is the area just above the medulla. It contains mostly white matter and provides a link between the cerebral cortex and the cerebellum. The midbrain is a small area above the pons that is involved in hearing and vision.

These three areas (medulla, pons, midbrain) are a part of the *lower* brain stem. The *upper* brain stem is the diencephalon, consisting of the thalamus and the hypothalamus. The thalamus is made up of gray matter and conducts all the sensory information (with the exception of smell) to the cerebrum. Below the thalamus is the hypothalamus, the control center for moods and motivation, sexual maturation, temperature regulation, and hormonal body processes.

OTHER AREAS OF THE BRAIN

Three other areas of the brain and central nervous system regulate body functions.

Optic Chiasma

Vision and the optic nerve

Pituitary Gland

Hormonal body processes
Physical maturation
Growth (height and form)
Sexual maturation
Sexual functioning

Spinal Cord

Conduit and source of sensation and movement

3

Causes of Alzheimer's Disease

Dr. Alois Alzheimer first discovered the "plaques and tangles" in the brain, but since then, researchers have found other changes that occur in the AD brain. Upon study of the AD brain, it shows consistent loss of neurons and synapses. Areas of particular loss are the forebrain, hippocampus, amygdala (area just beneath the surface of the front, medial part of the temporal lobe), and the cerebral cortex. There are four particular characteristics that define Alzheimer's disease:

1. Loss of neurons (especially cholinergic neurons)

2. Cortical atrophy—degeneration or withering of cerebral cortex

3. Presence of neurofibrillary tangles (NTs)

4. Accumulation of neuritic plaques (NPs)

A number of causes have been identified as relevant to the onset of Alzheimer's disease.

PLAQUES AND TANGLES

Neuritic plaques and neurofibrillary tangles are present in the AD brain. Scientists, however, do not know if they occur primarily because of the loss or death of neurons or if they occur secondarily as a result of the disease process. Plaques are lesions in the brain that are found outside of the cells, whereas NTs are found within the cells or neurons. NPs consist of a protein called **beta-amyloid protein,** which is enclosed by a mass of damaged neurons (Figure 3.1). NTs are inside the neuron and consist of a bundle of abnormally formed proteins called **tau proteins** (Figure 3.2). These abnormal formations of tau proteins within the cell disrupt normal cellular function and eventually lead to neuron death.

INFLAMMATION

Cytokines are proteins that play a role in both the body's immune system and in inflammation. Inflammation is thought to be another variable in the Alzheimer's process. This is because head injury or other major trauma to the brain is a known associated risk factor for AD. A study by the National Institute on Aging compared World War II veterans with head injury to those who did not. Preliminary information associated head injury with a risk of developing AD. Veterans who had mild head injuries with no skull fractures, and loss of consciousness for less than 30 minutes, had two times the risk of developing AD. Veterans who had head injuries that were more serious, those requiring hospitalization and who were unconscious for greater than 24 hours, had four times the risk of developing AD.

Cytokines are also thought to be neurotrophic, which means they may play a part in the growth and development of neurons. Therefore, research into medications to treat AD involves looking at cytokines and the inflammatory process along with their potential neurotrophic effect. Other inflammatory factors of particular interest are the cyclooxygenase (COX) enzyme and its products called prostaglandins. Excess amounts of these factors increase levels of glutamate, an amino acid that excites nerves and, when overproduced, is a powerful nerve killer.

OXIDATION

As beta-amyloid protein breaks down, it releases unstable chemicals called **oxygen free radicals**. Once released, oxygen

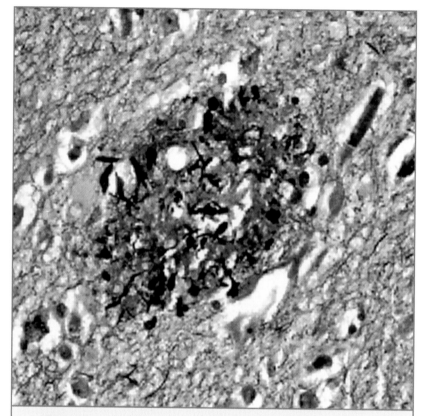

Figure 3.1 Neuritic plaques (NPs) are lesions in the brain that are found outside of the cells. Beta-amyloid plaques in an Alzheimer's brain (shown here) consist of proteins that are enclosed by a mass of damaged neurons.

free radicals bind to other molecules through a process called oxidation.

Oxidation is the result of many common chemical processes in the body, but when oxidants are overproduced, they can cause severe damage in cells and tissues, including affecting genetic material in cells (its DNA). Oxidation is known to play a role in many serious diseases, including coronary artery disease and cancers, and experts believe it may also contribute to Alzheimer's disease.

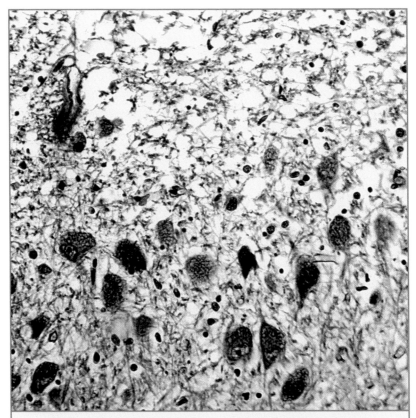

Figure 3.2 Neurofibrillary tangles (NTs) are found inside the neuron and consist of a bundle of abnormally formed proteins called tau proteins. These abnormal formations of tau proteins within the cell disrupt normal cellular function and eventually lead to neuron death.

CHOLINERGIC HYPOTHESIS

There are neurons that are vital to memory and cognition called cholinergic neurons. These neurons use **acetylcholine (ACh)**, a chemical transmitter, to stay vital. In normal aging, ACh decreases, causing short-term memory lapses. In AD, the decline in ACh can be around 90%. Some of the primary medications used in AD treatment are those that inhibit the breakdown of ACh.

MONOAMINE OXIDASE TYPE B

Monoamine oxidase type B (MAO-B) is found in human brain tissue and functions to metabolize (break down) dopamine and other neurotransmitters. Dopamine is essential to central nervous system functioning, and is responsible for movement and feelings of pleasure. It is thought that an increased amount of MAO-B is involved in Alzheimer's and is also associated with a rise in **oxidative stress** and oxygen free radicals.

GENETICS

Although Alzheimer's disease appears to have no specific or known cause, some cases may be genetic (inherited). There are a few specific genes that have been major targets of research. All of these genes seem to have some effect on beta-amyloid, either overproduction or destruction.

Apolipoprotein E (Apo E) is a gene that participates in the distribution of cholesterol for repairing nerve cells during development and after injury. The presence of this gene in humans appears to carry a risk of late-onset Alzheimer's (by age 85). This particular gene is located on chromosome 19.

Presenilin-1 and -2 (PS1 and PS2) gene mutations account for most cases of inherited early-onset AD (the fifth or sixth decade of life). This defective gene causes accelerated beta-amyloid plaque formation and cell destruction.

There is research that has identified other chromosome abnormalities that are precursors to Alzheimer's. One is Down syndrome (trisomy 21), in which there is an extra chromosome 21. Clinically, patients with this gene develop AD in the fifth decade of life. The other abnormality is gene factors on chromosome 10, which in the last few years has shown some causality to AD.

ESTROGEN LOSS

Estrogen is the primary female hormone (see "What are Hormones?" box). Research is attempting to determine if estrogen may have a protective effect against memory loss and lower mental functioning associated with normal aging. Laboratory studies have suggested that estrogen may block the production of beta-amyloid, the substance responsible for the plaque formation in AD brains. Estrogen may also trigger temporary nerve pathways in the brain, stimulate the production of the neurotransmitters ACh and serotonin (both depleted in AD brains), and increase blood flow to the brain. Finally, estrogen is an antioxidant and may clean up oxygen free radicals. Studies on how estrogen may relate to AD are still controversial.

ENVIRONMENTAL FACTORS

Research is being conducted on potential environmental causes of Alzheimer's disease. There have been some reports on the AD brain that have noted the presence of infectious organisms or heavy metals. Infectious organisms may be more likely to contribute to brain degeneration in persons genetically susceptible to AD. These organisms may increase inflammation or contribute to cell death. Exposure to certain metals has been another controversial factor in Alzheimer's research. Years ago, reports suggested that cooking in aluminum pots and pans or using deodorant containing aluminum could cause AD.

WHAT ARE HORMONES?

Hormones are a part of the endocrine system, one of the body's main systems for communicating, controlling, and coordinating the body's work. Hormones of the body's endocrine system work with the nervous system, reproductive system, kidneys, gut, liver, and fat to help maintain and control various activities in the body. The body's endocrine system controls energy levels, reproduction, growth and development, response to stress or injury, and our entire internal system (homeostasis).

Some laboratory reports have suggested that excessive amounts of zinc and copper have been observed in the AD brain. It is thought that these metals may alter the structure of beta-amyloid to a more harmful type. To this date, there is no substantiation for these theories.

SUMMARY

We've looked at the structure of the brain to see how Alzheimer's disease affects the functions of the brain and central nervous system. And we've seen that there are a number of potential factors considered as causes for AD. Finding the causes of Alzheimer's is essential in the search for a treatment. Once causes of AD are identified, it brings science that much closer to preventing Alzheimer's, slowing its progression, and even curing the disease.

4

Features and Diagnosis of Alzheimer's Disease

To understand the treatment strategies for Alzheimer's, it is valuable to know the various stages of the disease process and the diagnostic criteria. Research into AD is beginning to uncover the mysteries of this illness, allowing researchers to define at what point treatment should begin.

CHARACTERISTICS AND SYMPTOMS OF ALZHEIMER'S
It is often difficult to distinguish between normal decline in mental functioning due to aging and the onset of AD. There are fairly distinctive stages of AD, but it is important to realize that each individual with Alzheimer's can present with different combinations of characteristics. However, all have the general symptoms of decline in memory, functionality, and behavior.

STAGES OF ALZHEIMER'S DISEASE
Preclinical Alzheimer's:
The **entorhinal cortex** is the area of the brain in which AD begins. It forms the input to the hippocampus and is responsible for the pre-processing of input signals. The hippocampus is located in the temporal lobe of the brain and together with the entorhinal cortex is responsible for memory and navigation. Deterioration in these

areas probably occurs 10 to 20 years before signs or symptoms of AD are noted. These regions begin to atrophy (shrink) and memory loss is usually the first feature.

Mild cognitive impairment (MCI) is a condition that has similarities to preclinical AD. However, it is not entirely clear if they are identical. MCI is a condition characterized by mild recent memory loss, without dementia or significant impairment of other cognitive functions beyond that expected for age or educational background. The research suggests that many patients with MCI progress to AD. What is important about MCI is that this condition is increasingly being treated with AD medications in an attempt to slow down progression (or conversion) to AD or worsening function.

Mild Alzheimer's

With mild AD, the disease progresses and begins to affect the cerebral cortex. Memory loss continues and functioning begins to decline. Cognitive abilities, such as handling money and paying bills, becomes problematic. Other changes may include poor judgment, confusion about the location of familiar places (getting increasingly lost), loss of spontaneity or initiative, mood and personality changes, and increased anxiety.

These changes are because growing plaques and tangles are beginning to damage areas of the brain that control memory, language, and reasoning. An otherwise healthy, happy individual becomes moody or sullen. An intelligent, well-spoken person may increasingly be at a loss for words. Or a world traveler may be having difficulty returning from the neighborhood grocery store. Some individuals or family members may feel that these symptoms or signs may be part of the normal aging process. The realization that it may be more than that is often a difficult concept to grasp.

Moderate Alzheimer's

By the moderate stage of AD, the damage to the brain becomes more widespread. Areas of the cerebral cortex that control language, reasoning, and conscious thought become damaged. It becomes more evident that there is a problem. Behavior problems start to cause disruption in the Alzheimer patient's quality of life, as well as those around them. Problems such as wandering, agitation, and difficulty recognizing friends and family require more intense supervision. Other signs or symptoms include:

- Restlessness, anxiety, tearfulness

- Shortened attention span

- Increasing memory loss and confusion

- Difficulty with language (writing, reading, writing checks)

- Inability to learn or cope with new or unexpected situations

- Repetition in language or movements

- Inappropriate dressing for weather, sloppiness, vulgarity

- Paranoia, hallucinations, suspiciousness

At this stage, family members start to face some difficult decisions regarding the care of the patient. Arrangements need to be made for more intensive supervision, which often adds financial and emotional burdens.

Severe Alzheimer's

In this last stage of AD, the brain has atrophied (wasted away), and the plaques and tangles are throughout the brain (Figure 4.1). The patient is completely dependent on others. At this point, if financially able, even the most stoic family members will need to find a nursing home to take care of the AD patient. The patients usually cannot recognize family or loved ones, or communicate in any way. There is often weight loss, loss of bladder and bowel control, groaning and moaning, seizures, difficulty swallowing, and an increase in sleep. Most patients in this stage are bedridden, and frequently die from other illnesses. Aspiration pneumonia (a fatal lung illness that occurs by breathing food or liquids into the lung due to improper swallowing) is common due to lack of mobility.

DIAGNOSTIC CRITERIA

The only absolute confirmation of AD is to observe pathological changes in brain tissue. This can only be accomplished at autopsy. Otherwise, clinical presentation showing progressive deterioration in memory, function, and behavior, along with the elimination of other causes, confirms only "probable AD."

Criteria for AD established by the National Institute of Neurological and Communicative Disorders and Stroke--Alzheimer's Disease and Related Disorders Association (NINCDS-ADRDA) have improved the accuracy of diagnosis to approximately 90%. These criteria have become the standard for patients to enter clinical research trials for AD.

THE CASE OF CATHERINE, PART 1

Catherine was an 80-year-old Ukrainian immigrant, living with her widowed daughter and two grandsons. Catherine was the housekeeper and cook for the family, while her daughter worked and the grandsons were in school. Her family began to notice that this usually vibrant, charming woman was becoming irritable and forgetful.

The memory losses were not quite so noticeable until one afternoon when Catherine and her daughter were returning home from shopping. They were walking toward the house when Catherine stopped and refused to go in. She began insisting that this house was not hers. Other episodes of a similar nature prompted her daughter to take Catherine to her physician. Catherine was diagnosed with probable Alzheimer's disease and given a prescription for an AD medication.

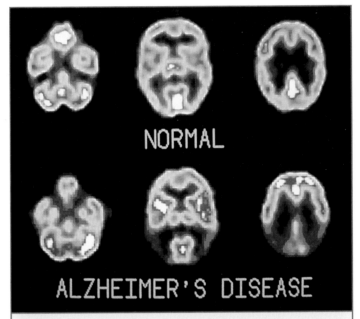

NORMAL

ALZHEIMER'S DISEASE

Figure 4.1 A positron emission tomography (PET) scan showing a normal brain compared with an Alzheimer's brain reveals the severe atrophy that takes place in the Alzheimer's brain. Plaques and tangles are scattered throughout the brain in the last stage (the most severe) of Alzheimer's disease.

A careful history is taken that includes signs and symptoms of AD described earlier. The history also includes a review of medications to rule out dementia caused by one of the medications. A review of trauma, depression, and family history is also necessary to rule out other potential causes of dementia. Deterioration in function and memory are assessed using various clinical evaluations that will be discussed shortly. Routine laboratory tests and a brain scan (neuroimaging) are also done to rule out stroke, tumors, and a **subdural hematoma** (a collection of blood that lies between the outer covering, the dura, of the brain and the brain's surface).

The American Psychiatric Association's *Diagnostic and Statistical Manual of Mental Disorders*, 4th edition, Text Revision

(DSM-IV-TR) also describes the diagnosis of AD. These criteria, similar to those of the NINCDS-ADRDA, describe a decline in functioning, while ruling out other possible causes. In addition, the DSM-IV-TR also divides the diagnosis of AD into two groups. "Early onset" is described as symptomatic clinical deficits beginning at age 65 or earlier. "Late onset" is the start of symptoms at an age older than 65 years.

CLINICAL ASSESSMENTS AND EVALUATIONS

There are several assessments used to assist in the diagnosis of AD. Not all are used at the same time, and some are utilized more in clinical trial settings as opposed to the physician's office. These evaluations help determine both a diagnosis and the progression of the disease. In clinical trials, it also helps determine the efficacy of the trial medication.

THE CASE OF CATHERINE, PART 2

The medication for Catherine did not seem to be working and she was becoming progressively worse. One day, the daughter and grandsons returned home to Catherine, who was, up until then, staying home alone, to find all the burners on the stove on full flame. At other times, she would throw the garbage out the door instead of in the trash can. It became apparent that her daughter had to stop working to take care of her mother.

The grandsons' lives were affected in various ways also. Since their mother stopped working, they started working themselves to save for college and a car. Many times, Catherine would wander off and they had to run around the neighborhood in a car or on foot to track her down. Sometimes, her antics were amusing, but most often they were emotionally wearing. She would repeatedly ask to be "taken home," so one grandson who tired of hearing this statement, took her to his car and said, "OK, Grandma, which way do we go?" Catherine responded stubbornly, "You know the way!" Her family often

Alzheimer's Disease Assessment Scale (ADAS)

The Alzheimer's Disease Assessment Scale (ADAS) is divided into noncognitive and **cognitive** (the mental process of knowing, including aspects such as awareness, perception, reasoning, and judgment) behavior subscales. The ADAS cognitive subscale (ADAS-cog) is the primary scale recognized by the United States Food and Drug Administration (FDA) to measure cognitive change. It is a scale containing 11 items with a range of possible scores from 0 to 70; higher scores reflect greater impairment. The noncognitive behavior scale is a 10-item scale with a range of possible scores from 0–50.

Mini-Mental State Examination (MMSE)

The Mini-Mental State Examination (MMSE) is a brief questionnaire that evaluates orientation, memory, attention,

mentioned how she would suddenly hush everyone and say, "The baby's crying."

Most of the other family members not in the immediate household did not have the patience to deal with Catherine's decline, so the daughter and grandsons got little relief in the day-to-day care of her. They would have to lock up the house to prevent her causing harm to herself. Knobs were taken off the stove, doors were locked, and the whiskey was hidden (she had turned into a heavy drinker). One day upon returning, they discovered that she nearly got herself out of the house by cutting around the lock using a butter knife.

Catherine did not decline to the point of being bedridden. Three years after she was diagnosed with AD, she passed away shortly after being diagnosed with pancreatic cancer at the age of 83. Interestingly, when the family was cleaning her favorite lounging chair to give it to charity, they found in the cushions all her medications that she was supposed to be taking to control her AD.

naming, comprehension, and implementation of a thought. Higher scores signify less impairment. It is widely used to assess diagnosis and to document changes. However, it has come under criticism for a few reasons. It is believed to be an inaccurate measure for patients who are elderly or with less education. These patients score lower initially, and reach zero while still deteriorating. In addition, this scale is criticized for lack of long-term reliability. Nonetheless, due to the brevity of the questionnaire and its familiarity to healthcare professionals, it is still commonly used.

GLOBAL ASSESSMENTS

These guidelines have been proposed by the FDA to assess clinically important changes that cannot be captured by quantitative questionnaires.

Clinician's Interview-Based Impression of Change (CIBIC)

The Clinician's Interview-Based Impression of Change (CIBIC) is a scale that is utilized by the physician while interviewing the patient. It is a standard questionnaire that is answered by the physician based on his or her perceptions of the patient's functioning. It is primarily used during clinical trials of medications.

Another scale utilized is the CIBIC with caregiver input (CIBIC-plus). This takes into account the impression of changes observed by the caregivers of the AD patient, who in all likelihood spend a greater amount of time with the patient.

Global Deterioration Scale (GDS)

The Global Deterioration Scale (GDS) is a seven-stage scale that does not require an interview with the patient. It follows the progression of disease using specific markers. A criticism of this scale is that a one-step change from one rating to another is not equivalent. An abridged version of this scale is depicted in Table 4.1.

Table 4.1 Global Deterioration Scale (abridged).

Stage 1	Normal	No memory deficit
Stage 2	Very mild	Complaints of memory deficit such as losing objects, or forgetting names.
Stage 3	Mild	Clear deficit that interferes with work or social activity.
Stage 4	Moderate	Decreased knowledge of personal history and current events. Can no longer handle finances or complex tasks. Denial and withdrawl may occur.
Stage 5	Moderately severe	Can no longer survive without assistance. Disoriented to time, poor recall, season matching clothing. No assistance needed with toileting/eating.
Stage 6	Severe	May forget name of spouse. Unaware of recent events in life, past sketchy. Changes in emotions, personality, sleep patterns. May be incontinent.
Stage 7	Very severe	All verbal abilities lost. Loss of walking. Incontinent. Unable to feed/toilet self. Reduced consciousness.

BEHAVIOR ASSESSMENTS

Disturbances in behavior are fairly common in Alzheimer's disease. These disturbances may include delusions, hallucinations, agitation, and depression. Behavior scales have not been used much in clinical settings or clinical trials for AD in the past. One reason is that most of the behavior scales are very narrow in scope and do not include the range of disturbances that can be seen in AD. However, in the late 1980s, there was an increased interest in measuring these disturbances during clinical trials, since recent findings suggested that some medications (cholinesterase inhibitors) used for AD can improve some behaviors. Two scales were developed for the specific purpose of measuring behavior in AD.

Behavior Pathology in AD
Rating Scale (BEHAVE-AD)

The Behavior Pathology in AD Rating Scale (BEHAVE-AD) scale rates 25 well-defined behaviors in seven different areas. These areas are:

1. Paranoid and delusional ideation

2. Hallucinations

3. Activity disturbances

4. Aggressiveness

5. Diurnal rhythm disturbances

6. Affective disturbance

7. Anxiety and phobias

Neuropsychiatric Inventory (NPI)

The Neuropsychiatric Inventory (NPI) scale was developed to evaluate the psychiatric disturbances of the patient with cerebral disease. It evaluates 12 different areas that are common in patients with AD:

1. Delusions

2. Hallucinations

3. Agitation

4. Dysphoria (an emotional state characterized by anxiety, depression, or unease)

5. Anxiety

6. Apathy (absence of emotion or enthusiasm)

7. Irritability

8. Euphoria (intense good feeling)

9. Lack of inhibitions

10. Aberrant motor behavior (abnormal movement, such as wandering)

11. Nighttime behavior disturbances

12. Eating and appetite disorders

ASSESSING THE CAREGIVER

In addition to evaluating the patient, the amount of caregiver stress may also be evaluated. There are a number of instruments that can be used for this evaluation.

- Caregiver Activity Survey (CAS)—A self-administered tool measuring time spent by a caregiver with a person with AD. The survey includes six areas of caregiving activities: communicating with the person, using transportation, dressing, eating, looking after one's appearance, and supervising the person. CAS also includes four demographic questions and uses a 24-hour time frame.

- Caregiver Burden Inventory (CBI)—A 24-item scale designed to assess the experience of caregivers of cognitively impaired older people. This multidimensional instrument assesses five areas of burden: time-dependence, developmental, physical, social, and emotional.

- Caregiving Burden Scale (CBS)—A 13-item scale that evaluates the stress related directly to caring for elderly patients with AD, dementia, or other psychological conditions. This scale contains two areas for scoring: relationship (a negative evaluation of the caregiver/receiver relationship) and personal consequences (a subjective measure of the impact of giving care).

Caregivers often need care themselves to relieve the stress associated with caring for a patient with Alzheimer's. Some common helpful suggestions include:

- Asking for help, even if it is for an hour, to get some "down time"

- Joining support groups and Webgroups

- Exercise

- Maintain a sense of humor

5

Cholinesterase Inhibitors

The cholinergic hypothesis for Alzheimer's disease led to the evaluation of methods to treat the cholinergic deficit in AD. That is, treatments that slow the decrease in the neurotransmitter acetylcholine (ACh), which is vital to the neurons for memory and cognition. The one method that has been the most successful to date is the inhibition of the **enzyme** (proteins that facilitate biochemical reactions) that breaks down acetylcholine. This leads to enhancement of cholinergic transmission.

Acetylcholine is produced in cholinergic neurons from choline and acetyl coenzyme A (CoA) by the action of the enzyme choline acetyltransferase. Acetylcholine is stored in vesicles (chambers) at the **presynaptic** (area located before the juncture where the nerve impulse must pass and excite the **postsynaptic neuron**) cell terminal (Figure 5.1). Acetylcholine is then released following excitation or depolarization, where it travels across the synapse to connect to receptors on the postsynaptic and presynaptic cells. The receptors that accept acetylcholine are called muscarinic and nicotinic receptors. The action on the postsynaptic receptor causes a nerve impulse, while the action on a presynaptic cell may cause an increase in acetylcholine release. However, acetylcholine is quickly inactivated (broken down) to acetyl and choline by an enzyme called acetyl-cholinesterase (AChE). This prevents the activation of the nerve impulse. Another cholinesterase present in mammals is butyryl-cholinesterase (BChE). Its function in humans is still not clear,

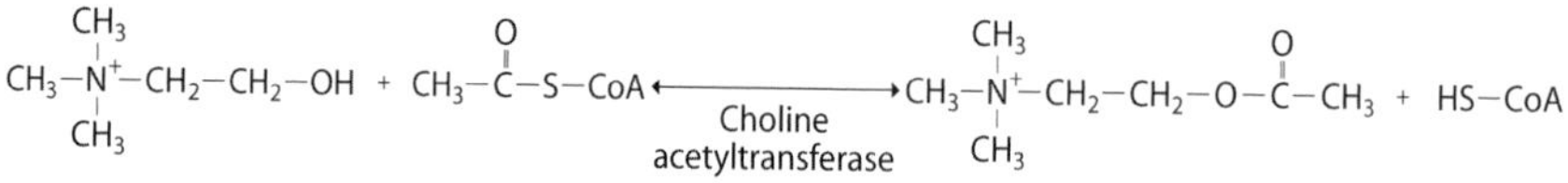

Choline **Acetyl CoA** **Acetylcholine** **Coenzyme A**

Figure 5.1 The neurotransmitter acetylcholine (ACh) is vital to the neurons for memory and cognition. Acetylcholine is produced in cholinergic neurons from choline and acetyl coenzyme A (CoA) by the action of the enzyme choline acetyltransferase.

although it is thought to serve as a "backup" when AChE activity is decreased or inhibited.

There are potentially other methods of increasing cholinergic activity, but they were not successful for several reasons. The attempt to use a drug that the body changed into acetylcholine failed to treat AD consistently. Drugs that were developed to activate the muscarinic or nicotinic receptors like acetylcholine either had too many side effects or did not work. The cholinesterase inhibitors are the medications that have improved symptoms of AD on a consistent basis with tolerable side effects. They are the first class of agents specifically approved by the United States Food and Drug Administration (FDA) for treatment of Alzheimer's disease.

HOW CHOLINESTERASE INHIBITORS WORK

The primary function of cholinesterase inhibitors (ChEI) is to inhibit the enzyme acetylcholinesterase (AChE), which breaks down acetylcholine. By inhibiting this enzyme, the effect is an increased level of ACh. It is, however, more complicated than a simple "cause and effect" reaction. The inhibition of AChE, thereby increasing acetylcholine, does not solve the problem of Alzheimer's. These inhibitors improve symptoms temporarily, and appear to slow the progression of Alzheimer's, but they do not cure AD. Alzheimer's disease has been shown to be complex and still not fully understood or explained.

The medications that are currently approved in the United States for treatment of mild to moderate AD are tacrine (Cognex), donepezil (Aricept), galantamine (Razadyne), and rivastigmine (Exelon). In general, each of the cholinesterase inhibitors have emerged as a class based on their action on the enzyme cholinesterase. These classes are reversible-inhibitors, pseudo-irreversible-inhibitors, and irreversible inhibitors. None of the approved drugs for AD are irreversible-inhibitors. The agents known as irreversible-inhibitors are typically organophosphate insecticides and are not approved for treating AD.

The reversible-inhibitors are tacrine, donepezil, and galantamine. They are considered "reversible" because they inhibit the enzyme for a short period of time, and then within minutes AChE is regenerated. These drugs are usually further defined as "short-acting" reversible inhibitors. Rivastigmine inhibits both acetylcholinesterase and butyrylcholinesterase (BChE) for a longer period of time (up to 10 hours). Rivastigmine is more stable than the other three drugs and is therefore considered an "intermediate-acting" reversible inhibitor. It is sometimes referred to as a pseudo-irreversible inhibitor, but this term is dropping out of favor.

TACRINE (COGNEX)

Tacrine was the first cholinesterase inhibitor approved by the FDA (in 1993) for the treatment of Alzheimer's disease. It inhibits both AChE and BChE, with slightly more inhibition of BChE. The **half-life** of the drug is about three hours, which determines how often a day it must be administered. Therefore, tacrine must be taken four times a day. Studies have demonstrated significant improvement in both cognition (ADAS-cog) and clinician assessment (CGIC) scores compared to a **placebo** (inactive pill, Figure 5.2).

Clinical studies, however, had a high discontinuation rate because of side effects. The side effects seen most often in the treatment groups, compared with the placebo group, were nausea, vomiting, diarrhea, and loss of appetite (anorexia). In addition, a significant number of patients taking tacrine in the studies experienced an increase in alanine aminotransferase (ALT), a liver enzyme that increases when a drug is toxic, of at least three times the upper limits of normal, compared with those taking placebo.

In clinical practice, tacrine is started at a dose of 10 milligrams (mg), four times daily (40 mg total daily dose), and is

CLINICAL TRIALS

A clinical trial is research that involves people. The trials are designed for many reasons, some of which are to study the safety and effectiveness of a new drug or to compare different drugs used for the same treatment. A patient can participate in a clinical trial if they meet the requirements set up by the study group. The study group can be a sponsor of the trial, such as a pharmaceutical company, a group of health-care professionals (commonly physicians), or both. There are usually criteria on the type of patient to be both included and excluded.

If the trial is "placebo-controlled," patients run the risk of being assigned a placebo (often a sugar pill) rather than the medication being researched. However, unless the study is comparing two or more drugs, it is better to have a control or placebo group. There are patients that report both positive and negative effects even when they are on the placebo. Therefore, having a placebo attempts to rule out this "placebo effect." For example, if 10% of the patients on medication increased by 40 mg a day no more frequently than every four weeks to a maximum daily dose of 160 mg (40 mg, four times daily). The blood alanine aminotransferase level must be monitored every other week beginning in the fourth week. If there is an elevation of the enzyme between two to three times the upper limits of normal, ALT monitoring should be increased to weekly until ALT returns to normal; if between three to five times the upper limits of normal, the dose should be reduced to the previous level and alanine aminotransferase should be monitored weekly until levels are back to normal. If ALT becomes elevated more than five times the upper limits of normal, tacrine must be discontinued. Patients may often be **rechallenged** successfully after alanine aminotransferase has returned to normal. However, because of the potential for

report nausea and 10% of the patients on placebo report nausea, it could be assumed that nausea is not an effect due to the medication since the difference between the two groups was zero.

If the trial is "randomized," there is an equal chance of being assigned to either group, thereby minimizing a risk of bias associated with the study. In other words, if patients are not randomly assigned to a group (specific type of treatment or placebo), then it is possible that there could be some bias by the person assigning the patient to a particular group. A study is also considered more favorable with many patients participating. The larger the study, the more likely it is a good representation of the general population being studied.

There are, of course, many other aspects taken into consideration in each individual trial. But large, randomized, placebo-controlled (or controlled by another medication) trials are considered to have more significance over other trials that do not have these factors.

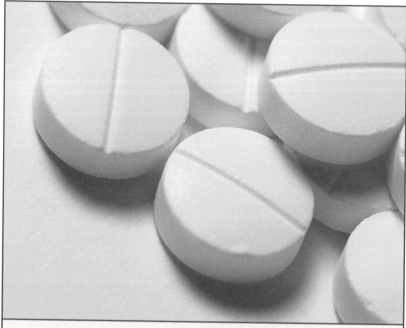

Figure 5.2 Placebos act as controls in clinical trials. Placebo pills often look identical to the medication being tested, but do not have the same chemical properties.

hepatotoxicity and the inconvenient dosing and laboratory monitoring schedule, tacrine has mostly dropped out of favor.

DONEPEZIL (ARICEPT)

Donepezil was approved by the FDA in 1996. It was the first drug to be referred to as a "second-generation" cholinesterase inhibitor. This reference was in large part due to the longer half-life of the drug (70 hours), requiring only once a day dosing. Once a day dosing is considered more favorable due to greater patient convenience, and therefore compliance, of the medication. Also, donepezil and the medications that follow do not have the liver toxicity issue associated with tacrine, making these second-generation drugs more tolerable and removing the need for inconvenient laboratory monitoring.

Donepezil was approved based on two large pivotal trials. Pivotal trials are clinical trials that meet the requirements of the FDA to show the safety and efficacy of a medication. There are four requirements to be considered a pivotal trial by the FDA:

1. Placebo controlled

2. Randomized (patients are given either medication or placebo in a random fashion)

3. **Double-blind design** when considered practical and ethical

4. Be of adequate size—lack of an adequate number of participants in a study is often a design flaw and makes the study less valid.

The donepezil trials demonstrated improved ADAS-cog and CIBIC-plus scores over placebo. Donepezil therapy is initiated at a dose of 5 mg once daily, usually taken in the evening, and is then increased to 10 mg once daily after six weeks, as tolerated. The most common side effects of donepezil in the clinical trials were nausea, diarrhea, muscle cramps, and abnormal dreams. These side effects occurred most often in individuals who were given an increased dosage of 10 mg a day after being on 5 mg a day for only one week. When the titration was lengthened to six weeks, the rate of side effects in the group taking 10 mg was virtually indistinguishable from that in the group on the lower dose.

RIVASTIGMINE (EXELON)

Rivastigmine was approved for use in the United States in 2000. Since it has a half-life of 10 hours, it allows for twice a day dosing. It is recommended that rivastigmine be given with meals to increase tolerability (decreases nausea and diarrhea). Dosing starts at 1.5 mg, twice daily, and increases every two weeks by 1.5 mg, depending on individual tolerability. Maximum dosage is 12 mg daily. Clinical experience has shown that a slower titration schedule increases tolerability.

Rivastigmine is known to have equal **affinity** (natural attraction) to inhibit AChE and BChE. What this means clinically is not yet known. Interestingly, in Alzheimer's disease, as AChE levels decrease in the brain and spinal fluid, BChE levels increase. So, one theory is that the metabolism of acetylcholine may become more dependent on BChE than AChE in Alzheimer's. Regardless, there are still higher levels of AChE than BChE, even if AChE is depleted. In addition, AChE is available closer to the synapse than BChE and probably plays a more important role in the breakdown of acetylcholine.

The most common side effects reported with rivastigmine are gastrointestinal (nausea and diarrhea). One of the benefits of rivastigmine appears to be minimal interactions with other medications. This means that there is less potential to have issues with patients taking multiple medications, a huge benefit in the elderly since they are commonly on multiple medications for various ailments.

GALANTAMINE (RAZADYNE)

Galantamine has been around for quite some time—it was first extracted from the European daffodil in the early 1950s. Since then, it has been made in the laboratory as galantamine hydrobromide and used all over the world as therapy for various neurological disorders. Some of these disorders are myasthenia gravis (a neuromuscular disorder that leads to progressive muscle weakness) and progressive muscle dystrophy (involving slow breakdown of muscles). Eventually, galantamine was approved for use in Alzheimer's disease in 2001.

Galantamine is a reversible inhibitor of acetylcholinesterase. An additional mechanism is as an allosteric modulator of nicotinic receptors—it enhances the response of these receptors to acetylcholine stimulation, although galantamine itself cannot stimulate the receptor; the clinical significance of this mechanism is not yet known. Its blood half-life and half-life of cholinesterase inhibition is approximately seven hours, and it is dosed twice daily. Dosing starts at 8 mg a day for four weeks, then 16 mg a day for four weeks, and finally to a maximum dose of 24 mg a day, as tolerated. As of 2005, there is an extended release product (Razadyne ER) available that is dosed once daily in 8 mg, 16 mg, or 24 mg capsules. The most common side effects of galantamine seen in clinical trials included nausea, vomiting, diarrhea, anorexia (loss of appetite), and weight loss.

WHICH MEDICATION TO CHOOSE?

In general, each of the above agents have similar effectiveness. There have been no trials to date that compare one cholinesterase inhibitor to another. Therefore, the initial medication is based on the individual patient. For example, a person who has minimal caregiver options may do better on donepezil or galantamine extended-release, since they are taken once daily. Another person may have multiple medications to take and therefore should take rivastigmine to avoid unnecessary drug interactions (Figure 5.3). Galantamine might be a better choice if a person suffers from abnormal or disturbing dreams.

Of course, any medication that is deemed intolerable should be stopped and another one tried. In addition, if a medication does not appear to be working after a reasonable time period agreed upon by the physician, it may be useful to try another medication. Patients who do not improve or otherwise respond to one medication in this class could potentially respond to another.

INITIATION OF THERAPY

At what point should a person with memory issues start taking medication? Should the person wait to be diagnosed with

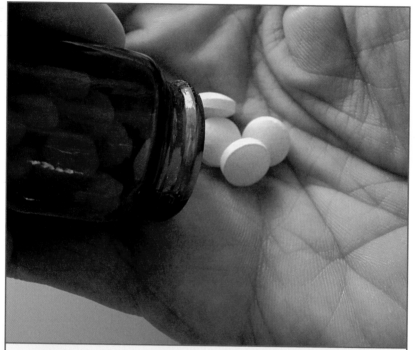

Figure 5.3 Medication is based on the individual patient. Some patients may be given multiple medications, while others may take only one type of drug. Precautions must be taken by the patient, doctor, and caregiver to avoid unnecessary drug interactions.

"probable AD"? How about medication for the patient with mild cognitive impairment (MCI)? What if an older person is starting to forget where he left his keys—should he be started on medication? These are difficult questions to answer and difficult to contrast and compare all of the clinical trials attempting to ascertain these answers. However, there are some important data emerging.

Clinical data has shown that Alzheimer's patients in similar stages of disease progression who were initiated on a cholinesterase inhibitor did not decline as rapidly as their counterparts who were on placebo. In addition, there is evidence that patients on higher doses or maximum doses do better than patients on lower doses. These data suggest that there may be ultimate benefit if the medication was started earlier in the disease. Studies are currently under way to determine whether the administration of cholinesterase inhibitors to individuals with isolated memory impairment can delay or prevent progression to Alzheimer's disease.

USING CHOLINESTERASE INHIBITORS

Even though it has not been fully established when to start therapy, studies are attempting to discern how long therapy should continue. Compared to the natural course of Alzheimer's disease, it appears that therapy is beneficial for several years. Cholinesterase inhibitors have also been noted to improve behavioral symptoms as AD progresses. In clinical studies, patients who stop therapy decline within several weeks and return to where their stage of progression would have been without therapy. If a patient needs to stop therapy for any reason, all attempts should be made to restart therapy as soon as possible. Restarting therapy after a lapse of more than 2–3 weeks shows benefit, but it may not be to the extent that would have been attained without stopping the medication or with less of a time lapse.

Several strategies are helpful in maximizing the benefit from the use of cholinesterase inhibitors in patients with Alzheimer's. Patients should be started on a ChEI as soon as the diagnosis is made. Dosages should be as slow as necessary to prevent the development of gastrointestinal or other side effects. Patients should also be given the highest dose they can tolerate. If they are not able to tolerate one of the medications, another agent should be considered. The risk of nausea can be reduced by administering the medication on a full stomach, and antiemetics (medications that minimize nausea) can be used if necessary. Patients should continue on the medication indefinitely (or until they no longer have meaningful interactions with other individuals), because it may still help alleviate behavior problems even when cognition is severely impaired.

SUMMARY

Cholinesterase inhibitors have been shown to prolong the time to severe impairment in patients with Alzheimer's disease, and their use is now considered to be the standard of care in its treatment. Several agents are now available, providing alternatives for treatment, along with the ability to individualize therapy. Although these agents are approved for the treatment of mild- to moderate-stage Alzheimer's, more recent data suggest that therapy should be started as soon as the diagnosis is made and that it may continue to benefit the patient even into the severe stages of the disease.

6

Novel Therapies

Even though the cholinesterase inhibitors have become the standard treatment for Alzheimer's disease today, the future of treatment is clearly directed toward new targets. These new targets are the actual plaques and tangles, as well as possible mechanisms that have yet to be discovered. Current therapies (other than the ChEIs) are in clinical trials and some therapies are still in drug discovery.

MEMANTINE (NAMENDA)

Memantine is approved for the treatment of moderate to severe Alzheimer's. It is an N-methyl-D-aspartate (NMDA) receptor antagonist. The NMDA receptor is one of several receptors located on the postsynaptic neurons in the hippocampus, which receive transmissions from the neurotransmitter **glutamate** (Figure 6.1). Glutamate is a major excitatory neurotransmitter that is associated with learning and memory, used by more than 80% of the neurons in the brain. Apart from the physiological role of glutamate, excessive activation of its receptors can also evoke neuronal dysfunction and even damage or death. This cell death ascribed to an excessive activation of glutamate receptors has been termed *excitotoxicity* and seems to occur in acute insults, such as stroke and trauma, but also in chronic neurodegenerative diseases such as AD.

In a normal brain, the NMDA receptor is blocked by magnesium ions, thereby protecting the neuron against **glutamatergic excitotoxicity.** During physiological learning and memory processes, high concentrations of synaptic glutamate are transiently released. In response to the presence of glutamate, **magnesium,** a

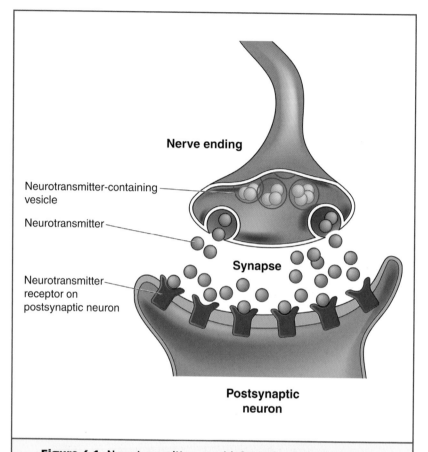

Nerve ending

Neurotransmitter-containing vesicle

Neurotransmitter

Synapse

Neurotransmitter receptor on postsynaptic neuron

Postsynaptic neuron

Figure 6.1 Neurotransmitters send information from the nerve ending by attaching to receptors on the postsynaptic neuron. Memantine is approved for the treatment of moderate to severe Alzheimer's. It is an N-methyl-D-aspartate (NMDA) receptor antagonist. The NMDA receptor is one of several receptors located on the postsynaptic neurons, which receive transmissions from the neurotransmitter glutamate.

mineral involved in various processes in the body, leaves the NMDA receptor. The exit of magnesium is due to a voltage change that has occurred within the cell. Calcium (another mineral affected by voltage) enters into the cell, and through secondary processes, the signal is recognized. In Alzheimer's, the pathological, sustained release of low glutamate concentrations, from both neurons and surrounding glial cells, displaces magnesium from the NMDA receptor channel. There is a continuous influx of calcium into the cell, increasing the calcium pool. In the case of learning and memory processes, the transient synaptic release of glutamate causes more calcium to flow into the cell. However, due to the already elevated calcium concentration, the signal can no longer be detected (leading to the occurrence of dementia symptoms). In the course of the disease, the chronic release of glutamate and the permanently increased intracellular calcium concentration leads to neuronal degeneration (Figure 6.2).

As memantine, in contrast to magnesium, blocks the NMDA receptor in the presence of the sustained release of low

HOW MEMORY WORKS

The fundamental characteristic of the human brain that makes learning and memory possible is its **plasticity,** the ability of the neurons to modify their connections to make certain neural circuits more efficient. The pathways along which information travels through the neurons of the brain can be compared with the paths through a forest. As people keep taking the same route through a forest, they wear out a path. And the more people take this path, the more deeply it is worn and the easier it becomes to follow. The same goes for our memories: the more we review them in our mind, the more deeply they are etched in our neural pathways. The brain is also "pre-wired" to learn some things effortlessly, such as what somebody's face looks like, while other things, such as theoretical mathematics, take more work. It all depends on the networks that already exist in our brains, which developed based on their usefulness during the evolution of our species.

Slowing the onset of Alzheimer's

Little is known about how and why Alzheimer's happens, but research indicates that there may be effective ways to prevent it or at least slow its progress.

A degenerative pattern

Alzheimer's works fast, reducing neuro-function significantly in just a few years. Positron Emission Tomography (PET) imagery, by measuring brain activity, has helped doctors reveal the areas of the brain most affected.

Normal brain - Red areas are highest in neuro-activity.

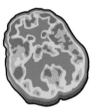

Alzheimer's afflicted brain - Eight years later, function is reduced by almost a third.

Getting a head start

Although there is little definitive research, a few theories on preventative measures are peaking interest:

 Estrogen and ginkgo biloba - Studies are underway that may link these substances to Alzheimer's prevention, possibly due to anti-inflammatory or circulatory properties.

 Anti-inflammatory drugs - Animal studies show these drugs can limit the production of amyloid, the protein deposits that are characteristic of an Alzheimer's afflicted brain.

 Statin drugs - Originally prescribed for high cholesterol, doctors observed that the drugs reduced Alzheimer's risk as well, leading many to draw a correlation between cholesterol levels and Alzheimer's disease.

 Folate - High levels of the amino acid homocysteine have been shown to increase risk of Alzheimer's and heart disease. The nutrient folate, already added to flour, is known to lower it.

 Mental exercise - Some believe that getting lots of mental activity can make the brain stronger and more equipped to function even if Alzheimer's attacks.

SOURCES: UCLA, David Geffen School of Medicine; Associated Press   **AP**

Figure 6.2 Alzheimer's is a degenerative disease. The disease causes neuroactivity in the brain to decrease over a period of time. The onset of Alzheimer's can be slowed or even prevented through certain drugs, diet, and mental exercise.

glutamate concentrations, the influx of calcium is prevented (**neuroprotection**). The intracellular calcium concentration is reduced. During learning and memory processes, memantine leaves the NMDA receptor for a short time. A signal is produced that is now recognized and processed, leading to a symptomatic improvement in dementia symptoms.

It is important to know that memantine is a low to moderate NMDA receptor blocker. Specifically, this means that it has an affinity (attraction) for the NMDA receptor on a low or moderate level as opposed to a high affinity. The importance of this is the fast-blocking and subsequent unblocking of the receptor, which allows for normal physiologic functioning (in this case, memory and learning). In addition, memantine appears to selectively inhibit the receptor while allowing some normal functioning. An added benefit is the minimal side effects. In clinical trials, the side effects most commonly reported with memantine included agitation, urinary incontinence (involuntary release of urine), and insomnia (inability to sleep), which occurred in similar rates in the placebo group.

A drug with high affinity, such as phencyclidine (PCP), produces severe side effects, including hallucinations, inability to walk, and memory loss. These drugs have also yielded poor clinical results. Due to the high affinity, these drugs have slow blocking/unblocking rates on the receptor and do not allow normal physiologic functioning.

The initial dose of memantine is 5 mg a day, then increased over several weeks to a recommended target dose of 20 mg daily (10 mg given twice a day). Results of several clinical studies demonstrated less global, functional, and cognitive decline in patients on memantine than patients on placebo. Study results have also shown that memantine was associated with a significantly lower rate of caregiver time-burden and placement of patients in an institution compared to the placebo group.

ANTIOXIDANTS AND SELECTIVE MONOAMINE OXIDASE INHIBITORS

Studies of the Alzheimer's brain post-mortem have found several markers of oxidative damage. The loss of neurons may cause oxidative stress and the release of oxygen free radicals (see "Oxidative Stress" box). **Antioxidants** have been studied as possible preventatives for AD and both vitamin E and C have been investigated. Vitamin E has shown some positive effects

OXIDATIVE STRESS

Oxidative stress is part of normal aging, but it also occurs in intoxicated individuals (alcoholics) to some extent, persons with metabolic abnormalities, and other conditions of physiologic stress where the balance of free radicals and antioxidants is thrown off.

Atoms consist of a nucleus, neutrons, protons, and electrons. Electrons are involved in chemical reactions and are the substance that bonds atoms together to form molecules. Electrons surround, or "orbit," an atom in one or more shells, and the most important structural feature of an atom for determining its chemical behavior is the number of electrons in its outer shell. A substance that has a full outer shell tends not to enter into chemical reactions (an inert substance). Because atoms seek to reach a state of maximum stability, an atom will try to fill its outer shell by:

- Gaining or losing electrons to either fill or empty its outer shell

- Sharing its electrons by bonding together with other atoms in order to complete its outer shell

Electrons are stable when they are in pairs. Normally, bonds don't split in a way that leaves a molecule with an odd, unpaired electron. But when weak bonds split, **free radicals** are formed. Free radicals are very unstable and but results remain controversial. In addition, there have been no definitive results showing either vitamin E or C as valuable in various stages of Alzheimer's. Still, many clinicians add vitamin E to a patient's regimen due to its ready availability, affordability, and the fact that it is a vitamin that is both harmless and potentially beneficial if taken in recommended doses.

Monoamine oxidase inhibitors (MAOIs) are consistently studied to determine their role in Alzheimer's treatment. These

react quickly with other compounds, trying to capture the needed electron to gain stability. Generally, free radicals attack the nearest stable molecule, "stealing" its electron. When the "attacked" molecule loses its electron, it becomes a free radical itself, beginning a chain reaction. Once the process is started, there is a domino effect resulting in the disruption of living cells.

Some free radicals arise normally during metabolism, and sometimes the body's immune system's cells purposefully create them to neutralize viruses and bacteria. However, environmental factors such as pollution, radiation, cigarette smoke, and herbicides can also spawn free radicals. Normally, the body can handle free radicals by using **antioxidants**, which are a part of a normal diet, but if they are unavailable or if the free-radical production becomes excessive, damage can occur. Of particular importance is that free radical damage accumulates with age.

Antioxidants neutralize free radicals by donating one of their own electrons, ending the electron-stealing reactions. The antioxidant nutrients don't become free radicals by donating an electron because they are stable in either form. The antioxidants act as scavengers, helping to prevent cell and tissue damage that could lead to disease. The two most studied antioxidants are vitamins C and E.

are substances that inhibit the enzyme monoamine oxidase. Up to this point, the benefit remains to be seen.

Monoamine oxidase (MAO) is an enzyme that breaks down certain neurotransmitters, including dopamine, serotonin, and norepinephrine. MAOs are widely distributed throughout the body and their concentration is especially high in the liver, kidneys, stomach, intestinal wall, and brain. There are two forms of monoamine oxidase, MAO-A and MAO-B. In humans, intestinal MAO is predominantly type A, while most of that in brain is type B. Monoamine oxidase B (MAO-B) works in the brain to help recycle neurotransmitters. MAO-B and MAO-A work together to remove molecular pieces from neurotransmitters, part of the process of inactivating them. But along with this inactivation comes oxidative stress.

Scientists have developed drugs to block the actions of MAO enzymes, and by doing so, help preserve the levels of neurotransmitters in people with such disorders as Parkinson's disease and depression. Inhibition of the MAO-A enzyme in the central nervous system is responsible for the antidepressant action of the MAOIs. MAO-B increases with aging and patients with Alzheimer's show an increase in brain MAO-B levels above those observed as a result of normal aging.

Selegiline is a selective inhibitor of MAO-B. It has been used primarily in treating Parkinson's disease, but has been studied for use in Alzheimer's. Based on the mechanism of MAO-B inhibitors, which prevents the degradation of neurotransmitters, studies were conducted to see if they would benefit AD patients. Results have been mixed, with data showing some improvement in cognition, behavior, and mood. None of the studies have shown a significant enough effect to warrant their use. Selegiline also has antioxidant properties, but studies with vitamin E and selegiline compared to placebo did not show significant benefit in AD. In fact, studies with vitamin E showed a slight superiority over selegiline.

MAO inhibitors also have many undesirable side effects. Tremors, increased heart rate, and problems with sexual function are some of the mild side effects of MAO inhibitors, but more serious problems include seizures, large dips in blood pressure, and difficulty breathing. People taking MAOIs cannot eat foods containing the substance tyramine, which is found in wine, cheese, dried fruits, and many other foods. Most of the side effects occur because the drugs that attach to MAO enzymes do not have a perfect fit for either MAO-A or MAO-B.

ANTI-INFLAMMATORIES

Inflammatory mediators (substances in the body that produce an inflammatory response) are present near plaque formations in Alzheimer's disease. This suggests that the immune system may play an active role in the disease. These inflammatory mediators have been shown to increase beta-amyloid protein toxicity and free radicals, which accelerate the neurodegenerative process. Therefore, the interest in anti-inflammatory drugs is driven by two general observations. First, researchers have noted that chronic inflammation in the brain may contribute to nerve damage. Second, observational studies have shown that groups of people who take large doses of nonsteroidal anti-inflammatory drugs (NSAIDs) for such conditions as arthritis have a reduced likelihood of developing AD.

NSAIDs include aspirin and aspirin-like compounds that are generally used to treat pain, inflammation, and fever. They inhibit the function of enzymes involved in the immune system's inflammatory response. NSAIDs are sold in over-the-counter and prescription dosages. However, chronic and excessive use of these drugs can lead to potential side effects, such as irritation of the stomach lining, gastric bleeding, heart attack, stroke, and other serious complications.

Studies conducted using NSAIDs in patients with probable AD have not shown significant results. Clinical studies conducted with a goal of determining if NSAIDs could prevent Alzheimer's have been controversial. Some of the issues that have surfaced are which NSAID works better (patients respond differently to different NSAIDs), how long they should be taken, at what dose, and at what point to begin treatment.

There has been no complete clinical evaluation of NSAIDs that would recommend their use to prevent Alzheimer's. The prolonged use of any medication can have serious side effects and should be discussed with a physician. Ongoing laboratory studies and clinical trials will help researchers determine the appropriate use of NSAIDs as a treatment or prevention option.

ESTROGEN

Estrogen may also play a protective role against neuron damage. The observation that women appear to be at greater risk for Alzheimer's disease than men has sparked the interest of clinical investigators. In addition, large epidemiologic (the study of the transmission, incidence, and frequency of disease) studies have shown the risk of developing AD to be reduced in women on estrogen supplementation. Estrogen is thought to protect the brain by promoting neuronal growth and preventing oxidative damage. Testosterone, the male hormone, converts to estrogen in the brain. Testosterone levels do not decline as drastically in aging men as estrogen does in women during menopause. This may be one explanation for fewer incidences of Alzheimer's in men.

There have been no studies showing any significant benefit in taking estrogen for AD. In fact, results from a large trial called the Women's Health Initiative (WHI) study showed that women who were on an estrogen-progestin combination had an increased risk of breast cancer, heart disease, stroke, blood clots, and dementia. Women taking estrogen alone had an increased risk of stroke. Neither estrogen alone nor estrogen-progestin prevented women from getting dementia or mild cognitive impairment (MCI).

It appears that estrogen may not be a benefit for prevention of Alzheimer's, but it is still too early to make that
determination. Estrogen use for treating AD has not been
determined. There may be other differences between women
who choose to take estrogen and those who do not. For
instance, some women may receive better medical care. These
attributes together or alone may be what decreases their risk
of AD. It is also possible that estrogen may play a role in
combination with other medications. However, as of now, the
risks appear to outweigh the benefits of estrogen use.

ANTI-LIPID (CHOLESTEROL) THERAPY

As mentioned in Chapter 3, Apo E functions as a carrier for
cholesterol in the blood and central nervous system. In the
brain, it is important for distributing cholesterol for repair of
neuronal membranes and myelin. Thus, production of Apo E
increases when there is injury of neuronal tissue. The gene
responsible for production of Apo E is on chromosome 19,
the region previously discussed that is associated with late-
onset Alzheimer's disease. Of the three types of Apo E
(Apo E2, Apo E3, and Apo E4), Apo E4 is the one that puts
a person most a risk for the late-onset AD. These genetic
tendencies are inherited, but the degree of risk depends on
other factors, such as age, ethnicity, gender, and how many
copies (one from one parent or one from each parent) of the
gene are passed on. One gene copy may or may not increase
the risk, and inheriting two copies does not automatically
doom a person to Alzheimer's.

Attempting the use of cholesterol-lowering therapies
makes sense and some studies have shown promise. The
products tried most often are the HMG-CoA-reductase
inhibitors, otherwise known as the statins. The statins have
become the primary medication used for high cholesterol.
The statins inhibit the enzyme HMG-CoA-reductase responsible for **catalyzing** (initiating or accelerating) the reaction

of reducing HMG-CoA to mevalonate. This is considered the rate-limiting step in cholesterol synthesis. Several steps after mevalonate formation, cholesterol is synthesized, which means produced from several products or reactions (Figure 6.3).

In addition to their lipid-lowering properties, the benefit of statins is believed to be "protective" for Alzheimer's. It is not completely understood but there appears to be some alteration of the B-amyloid protein as well as other mechanisms. Unfortunately, no clinical trials have demonstrated efficacy in the prevention or treatment of AD. The good news is that with the information known at this time, there may be future lipid-lowering treatments designed to address Alzheimer's directly.

NERVE GROWTH FACTORS

Nerve growth factors are a type of gene therapy being investigated for treating Alzheimer's. They are proteins that regulate nerve cell maturation, survival, and repair. Clinical trials are in the very early stages, so these therapies are not yet available for treatment. Gene therapy (sometimes called gene transfer) is a medical technique being studied for a number of diseases, such as cancer, Parkinson's disease, and cystic fibrosis. It is a technique that uses genes to treat diseases: genes are transferred or added to cells so that the body can make a protein to fix a disease.

At this time, there are no Food and Drug Administration (FDA) approved gene transfer products for the treatment of any illness. Gene transfer for Alzheimer's is experimental and involves an investigational drug that stimulates the production of nerve growth factors. It is given through a surgical procedure in which a neurosurgeon precisely injects the investigational drug through a needle inserted into the area of the brain that is affected by Alzheimer's. This type of procedure is very risky and is certainly not as simple as taking a pill. However, these procedures hold a lot of promise for treatment in the future.

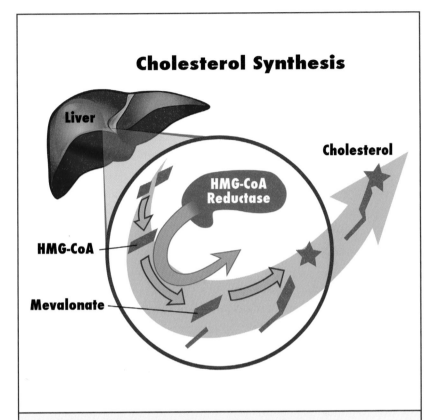

Figure 6.3 During cholesterol synthesis, the enzyme HMG-CoA-reductase helps convert HMG-CoA into mevalonate.

ANTI-AMYLOID THERAPIES

A theory that has generated a lot of discussion is the "amyloid hypothesis." Proponents of the amyloid hypothesis see production and aggregation of beta-amyloid as the key event in the nerve cell disruption and destruction seen in Alzheimer's disease. So far, two potential therapeutic approaches have been identified. One approach relies on various strategies for stimulating an immune system response that destroys beta-amyloid. The first **immunotherapeutic** compound to reach clinical trials, the "Alzheimer vaccine," failed to fulfill its early promise. Even though that trial failed, the effort may still yield valuable insights into beta-amyloid and its role in AD, as well as point the way to refinements of this type of approach.

The second amyloid targeting strategy inhibits the enzymes called secretases that cut amyloid precursor protein (APP) into successively smaller pieces, ultimately producing beta-amyloid. Secretases are classified as proteases, the same category of enzymes targeted by the protease inhibitors that have revolutionized AIDS therapy. A number of pharmaceutical companies are developing secretases and the first such drug has reached clinical trials.

STEM CELLS

Stem cells can be described as the body's self-repair kit: they have the potential to develop into many different cell types in the body. Theoretically, stem cells can divide without limit to replenish and repair brain cells, muscle cells, nerve cells, and red blood cells—possibly all the types of cells that exist in the body.

Stem cell research is a political, ethical, and moral controversy that has and will create volatile discussions for a long time. The major issue is that stem cells are harvested from human **embryos** (the pre-fetal stage from conception through the eighth week of development). Embryonic stem cells are thought to have much greater developmental potential than adult stem cells. It is the ability of the embryonic cell, in theory, to become all types of tissues that offers hopes of a cure for so many diseases. As you can imagine, the use of a human embryo for research is a huge controversy. The other issue, particularly in Alzheimer's research, is that the cause and progression of AD is not yet fully understood. Therefore, the use of stem cells continues to be only a theoretical option.

NON-PHARMACOLOGIC THERAPY
Ginkgo biloba

Ginkgo is an herbal extract that has been claimed to improve memory (see "The Ginkgo Tree" box). It is considered an antioxidant, anti-inflammatory, and an agent to improve blood flow, but these claims have yet to be demonstrated through large, randomized, placebo-controlled trials. Smaller trials have compared ginkgo to placebo in Alzheimer's patients and have shown some improvement in cognition and social behaviors. However, these studies were difficult to access because of a lack of patients who finished the study and too small a study group to show significance.

The media, and subsequently many marketers, have utilized this information to create a lot of frenzy over this product. The fact remains that this is an herbal product that is not controlled through a centralized agency such as the

THE GINKGO TREE

Ginkgo biloba is the last surviving member of the Ginkgoaceae family. It has existed essentially unchanged for several hundred million years. This tree was alive in forests throughout the world in its current form when the dinosaurs roamed the Earth. Because of this longevity, Charles Darwin referred to Ginkgo biloba as a "living fossil." Some of the oldest fossil forest remnants are at Ginkgo Petrified Forest State Park in Washington.

Ginkgo plants are either male or female. The female ginkgo fruits upon maturity at age 20 or later. When the protective layer for the seed decays on the ground, it releases a distinctly unpleasant aroma variously described as being like rancid butter or vomit. As a result, many avoid planting female trees along public streets. However, the seed itself is highly prized in traditional Chinese medicine. Extracts from the leaves of the ginkgo tree have been used as Chinese herbal medicine to treat a variety of medical conditions.

FDA. Therefore, the amounts of active ingredient in each product vary from batch to batch and manufacturer to manufacturer. In addition, there are no standards on appropriate dosing. Finally, there are no data on the effects on humans with long-term use. Side effects have been reported, such as diarrhea, nausea, headaches, increased bleeding, and bruising.

INTERVENTIONS

There are many interventions or therapies that can be utilized to improve the quality of life of both the Alzheimer's patient and the caregivers. These interventions may also potentially prolong memory and reduce behavioral and mood symptoms. One approach is the three R's—repeat, reassure, and redirect. The caregiver repeats answers to questions or repeats familiar stories. Such an intervention was depicted in the film *The Notebook*. James Garner played the husband whose spouse (Gina Rowlands) had Alzheimer's disease. He read from his wife's notebook every day in an effort to spark her memory. Reassuring an AD patient can go a long way toward reducing their anxiety. When it appears that a patient's behavior may get out of control, redirecting the patient to another activity may dissolve the problem.

Routine is another common intervention for AD patients. Keeping them on an eating and sleeping schedule, along with other planned activities, reduces anxiety and increases their comfort level.

Exercise (as long as it is physically possible for the AD patient) has been shown to improve mood, increase appetite, and increase the sense of well-being. Also, insure a safe environment by eliminating throw rugs, increase lighting, and minimize sharp objects.

Other helpful suggestions include:

- Keep recognizable personal objects and clothing for patient

- Simplify tasks by breaking them down into several shorter tasks

- Equip the patient's environment with safety locks

- Keep the AD patient oriented to time and place by displaying clocks and calendars

- Avoid loud noises and other excessive stimulation

Caregivers should also consider finding help, such as friends, relatives, or adult day-care programs, to relieve the stress on them.

7
Adjunctive Treatments

Adjunctive treatment is medicine or supportive interventions that usually are a part of the overall treatment of Alzheimer's disease but not the main treatment. As AD progresses, there are often behavior symptoms that accompany the memory deficits. These behavior symptoms tend to fall into one of three categories—psychosis, agitation, and depression. These symptoms may come and go, and they may differ among patients with AD. Just as treatment for memory can be a combination of medication and supportive interventions, so can the treatment for these behavior symptoms.

PSYCHOSIS

Psychotic symptoms can include paranoia (unfounded or exaggerated distrust of others), delusions (mistaken or unfounded opinion or belief), and hallucinations (hearing things, seeing things, or both). Antipsychotic agents should only be used if the psychosis becomes unmanageable for the caregiver or harmful to the patient. If the delusions, hallucinations, or paranoia do not harm anyone, then supportive interventions are recommended instead of medication. This is because antipsychotics do not cure the patient of these symptoms, and the side effects from the medications are sometimes troubling.

The antipsychotics used in Alzheimer's are the same medications that are used in **schizophrenia**, most often atypical antipsychotics. Two of the medications used most commonly in AD patients are risperidone and quetiapine. These newer atypicals tend to have fewer side effects compared to their older counterparts, sometimes referred to as "first generation" antipsychotics. The first generation medications that tend to be more commonly mentioned with Alzheimer's are haloperidol and thioridazine. Together, both the first generation medications and the newer atypical antipsychotics have also been labeled "major" or "minor" tranquilizers. The minor tranquilizers are primarily used for agitation or sleeplessness (insomnia) and will be discussed in the agitation section. The major tranquilizers are what we just referred to as the antipsychotics. These medications should be carefully followed by a medical professional.

Side effects appear to be more troubling in Alzheimer's patients since most are elderly. The elderly are more sensitive to these types of medications (Figure 7.1). Side effects most often observed were involuntary body movements, drowsiness, dizziness, confusion, dry mouth, and low blood pressure when going from a sitting position to standing, which may cause fainting. Therefore, doses in the elderly should be started low and increased slowly.

AGITATION

Agitation in Alzheimer's disease, manifested by irritability, restlessness, physical and verbal aggression, and aimless wandering, is a frequently encountered management problem. The mechanisms of agitation are not known. The problem occurs in approximately 80% of patients and seriously affects the patient's quality-of-life and his or her caregivers' level of stress. A variety of interventions, both non-pharmacologic and pharmacologic, have been used to manage agitation in AD.

Non-pharmacologic treatment options for agitation and aggression have focused on calming therapy, massage, baths, and music for patients, as well as education and protective techniques for caregivers. Pharmacologic interventions include antidepressants and minor tranquilizers. Antidepressants will

Figure 7.1 The elderly are more sensitive to some types of tranquilizers used to treat Alzheimer's. Some common side effects of tranquilizers include drowsiness, dizziness, confusion, dry mouth, and low blood pressure.

be discussed in the next section. The tranquilizers that are frequently used are a class of medications called the benzodiazepines, such as lorazepam (Ativan) and diazepam (Valium).

DEPRESSION

The incidence of depression in Alzheimer's patients is difficult to accurately determine. The percentage of incidence has been estimated anywhere from 10% to 80%. Part of the problem with accurate determination of depression is that the elderly suffer from depression without having AD. Secondly, it is difficult to differentiate the symptoms of Alzheimer's from depression. Lack of expression, loss of appetite, and difficulty concentrating can be symptoms of AD or depression. One of the ways to make a more accurate diagnosis is to determine if the patient is able to experience pleasure. Finally, depression may be more common in the early stages of Alzheimer's, when the patient is more aware of the loss of memory and declining ability to do daily tasks.

The medications commonly used for depression are antidepressants. Caution needs to be exercised in the elderly since they are more vulnerable to side effects, such as sleepiness, dizziness, agitation, and confusion. One class of antidepressants that tend to have a favorable side effect profile is the selective serotonin reuptake inhibitors (SSRIs). The neurotransmitter serotonin and the hormone noradrenaline in the brain are involved in control of the sleep/wake cycle, emotions, mood, arousal, emotion, drive, temperature regulation, and feeding. Thus, if a person has too little serotonin and noradrenaline in the part of the brain that controls mood, this will produce too little activity and that part of the brain becomes slower and less effective. This will lower mood.

In depression, it is known that there are reduced levels of both serotonin and noradrenaline. If too little serotonin (or noradrenaline) produces the symptoms of depression, then correcting this imbalance should help to reduce the symptoms. One way of doing this is to block the reuptake (recycling) of neurotransmitters (Figure 7.2). This is just what an SSRI antidepressant does: it blocks the reuptake of serotonin, so the next time an impulse comes along, there are more neurotransmitters, a stronger message is passed, and activity in that part of the brain is increased. Examples of SSRIs are fluoxetine (Prozac), sertraline (Zoloft), and paroxetine (Paxil).

NEUROTRANSMITTERS:
Keeping the Balance

Neurotransmitters are molecules that carry signals in the brain between neurons. When responding to situations, such as happiness, sadness, anxiety or fear, neurotransmitters are always active. Researchers are not yet sure exactly how neurotransmitters affect our feelings. However, clinical studies show that proper balance of neurotransmitters is critical to overall emotional well being. Emotional disorders like anxiety, depression and ADHD have all been linked to a chemical imbalance of specific neurotransmitters. This chemical imbalance can be caused by either an excess of neurotransmitter activity, or more commonly, a deficiency of neurotransmitter availability. Neurotransmitters are believed to have two functions; excitatory or inhibitory. Neurotransmitters with excitatory properties promote the initiation of nerve impulses in the receiving neuron. Neurotransmitters with inhibitory properties inhibit the initiation of nerve impulses.

When chemical imbalances in anxiety and depression are prevalent, researchers have found that neurotransmitters like serotonin, norepinephrine, dopamine and GABA may be unbalanced, usually in deficient amounts.

A process called reuptake is important in the understanding of how neurotransmitters work and why prescription drugs or alternative medicines are sometimes prescribed to help relieve anxiety or depression. *Reuptake*, or *uptake*, is a chemical process that occurs in the brain. It is defined as the reabsorption of a neurotransmitter *after* it has performed its function of transmitting a neural impulse. Therefore, once the neurotransmitter is reabsorbed it is no longer available in the active synapses of the brain. The function of the medications known as selective serotonin reuptake inhibitors (SSRIs) is to slow down the reuptake process. By doing so, there is temporarily more serotonin available in the brain, which improves a chemical imbalance, and therefore improves depression.

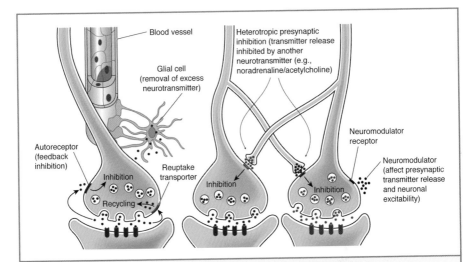

Figure 7.2 Neurotransmitters are recycled through a process called reuptake. Through the process of reuptake, the entire neurotransmitter molecule is reabsorbed through the end of the axon that originally released it. This process of reabsorbtion removes the neurotransmitter from the synaptic cleft so it cannot bind to receptors.

Another class of antidepressants that are commonly used in treating Alzheimer's disease is the tricyclic antidepressants (TCAs). The TCAs are just as effective as the SSRIs, but they have been associated with more side effects, such as cardiovascular (heart) effects, sedation, urinary retention, and dry mouth. In AD patients, the secondary amine TCAs (desipramine and nortriptyline) are recommended over the tertiary amine TCAs (amitriptyline and imipramine), due to fewer side effects.

LOOKING TO THE FUTURE

To understand Alzheimer's disease and memory drugs, it is necessary to have a background in the brain and its functions. Within the brain there is a complex network of neurons, neurotransmitters, synapses, hormones, elements, and many other components. Any number of mechanisms can fail, switch

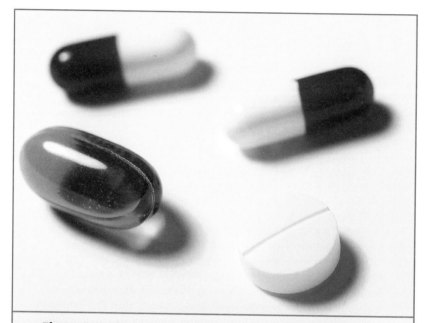

Figure 7.3 Alternative medications may be added to therapy as AD progresses, but it, too, is not a prevention or cure. Physicians may try a combination of ChEIs with vitamin E, *Ginkgo biloba*, or memantine.

off, degenerate, or be altered. The human brain is an amazing entity that can accomplish amazing things, and yet can create havoc when it fails. Alzheimer's disease is one failing that has yet to be completely understood.

Due to the complexity of AD and many of the unsolved mysteries of the disease, research will continue to unravel new discoveries for prevention and treatment. There are opportunities to discover new approaches, along with other therapies to improve memory or inhibit the destruction of memory.

The cholinesterase inhibitors (ChEIs) have proven to be helpful, but do not prevent or cure Alzheimer's. Namenda is another alternative medication to add to therapy as AD progresses, but it too is not a preventative or cure. Another approach is the combining of therapies and treatments. Most physicians will try a combination of treatments to get maximum results. For example, all of the interventions should be utilized with AD patients in addition to medication. Most Alzheimer's patients will start therapy with the ChEIs, due to their proven track record, and add vitamin E, *Ginkgo biloba*, or memantine depending on the patient (Figure 7.3). Patients or caregivers should not add vitamins or herbals on their own unless discussed with a physician.

The bright spot is the ongoing research in this area, and the potential possibilities that are getting closer to our grasp. Treatment options are furiously being researched and will hopefully provide additional options for Alzheimer's patients in the near future. With every discovery of brain function and its affect in Alzheimer's disease comes another chance to find a way to prevent and cure this devastating illness.

Glossary

Acetylcholine (ACh)—A chemical transmitter used by neurons.

Affinity—A natural attraction.

Antioxidants—Substances that help to neutralize oxygen free radicals in the body.

Beta-amyloid protein—A toxic protein that attacks the brain's nerve cells, affecting memory and learning.

Cerebral cortex—The outer layer of the brain responsible for numerous functions, such as movement, perception, memory, and speaking.

Cognitive—The mental process of knowing, including aspects such as awareness, perception, reasoning, and judgment.

Cortical atrophy—Degeneration or withering of the cerebral cortex.

Cytokines—Proteins that play a role in both the body's immune system and in inflammation.

Differential diagnosis—To rule out other causes.

Double-blind design—Both the patient and the physician are not made aware of who is on active medication and who is on placebo.

Embryo—The pre-fetal entity, from conception through the eighth week of development.

Entorhinal cortex—An important memory center in the brain, it forms the input to the hippocampus and is responsible for the pre-processing of the input signals.

Enzyme—Proteins present in the cells of all living beings that facilitate naturally occurring biochemical reactions.

Epilepsy—A disorder characterized by transient but recurrent disturbances of brain function that may be associated with impairment or loss of consciousness and abnormal movements or behavior.

Free radical—An unpaired, unstable atom that causes disruption of a living cell.

Glial cells—Cells that provide support and nutrition to the neurons.

Glutamate—A major excitatory neurotransmitter that is associated with learning and memory.

Glutamatergic excitotoxicity—Cell death ascribed to an excessive activation of glutamate receptors.

Half-life—The time required for half the quantity of a drug deposited in a living organism to be metabolized or eliminated by normal biological processes.

Hepatotoxicity—Toxic or dangerous to the liver.

Huntington's disease—A condition that results from genetically programmed degeneration of brain cells in certain areas of the brain. This degeneration causes uncontrolled movements, loss of intellectual faculties, and emotional disturbance.

Immunotherapeutic—Treatment or prevention of a disease using the body's immune system.

Magnesium—One of the minerals in the body responsible for biochemical reactions.

Metabolism—A process that creates energy by breaking down chemicals and nutrients.

Neuritic plaque—A diagnostic feature of Alzheimer's, they are extracellular abnormalities involving the accumulation of beta-amyloid proteins.

Neurofibrillary tangles—A diagnostic feature of Alzheimer's, they are composed of a hyperphosphorylated form of the microtubular protein tau.

Neurologist—A medical doctor who specializes in the brain and the disorders that affect the brain.

Neurons—Nerve cells that make up the nervous system and allow different parts of the body to communicate with each other.

Neuropathology—The study of the causes, nature, and effects of brain diseases.

Neuroprotection—A substance that has some protective features of the neurons (protects the neurons from toxicity).

Neurotransmitters—Chemical messengers by which neurons communicate with one another.

Oxidative stress—The steady state level of oxidative damage in a cell, tissue, or organ, caused by free radicals.

Oxygen free radicals—Unstable atoms with an oxygen center.

Placebo—Inactive pill or other route of administration that is given to patients or study participants unknowingly to assure unbiased results compared to medication.

Plasticity—The ability of the neurons to modify their connections to make certain neural circuits are more efficient.

Postsynaptic neuron—The receiving neuron located on the cell across the synapse.

Presynaptic—Area located before the synapse juncture where the nerve impulse must pass and excite the postsynaptic neuron.

Glossary

Pseudosclerosis—Caused by deposition of excess copper causing jaundice, tremors, vomiting, and slow, stiff movements.

Rechallenged—Medicine is attempted a second time.

Schizophrenia—Any of a group of psychotic disorders usually characterized by withdrawal from reality, illogical patterns of thinking, delusions, and hallucinations, and accompanied in varying degrees by other emotional, behavioral, or intellectual disturbances.

Subdural hematoma—A collection of blood on the surface of the brain. It lies beneath the outer covering (the dura) of the brain and the brain's surface.

Synapse—The gap between neurons.

Syphilis—A sexually transmitted infection (STI) caused by a bacterium called *Treponema pallidum*.

Tau proteins—Proteins that are expressed in neurons.

Notes

1. Alzheimer's Association. "Fact Sheet: About Alzheimer's Disease Statistics." *Alzheimer's Association*. Available online at http://www.alz.org.

2. Alzheimer's Disease Research. "The Facts on Alzheimer's Disease." *American Health Assistance Foundation*. Available online at http://www.ahaf.org.

Bibliography

Allain, H, D. Bentué-Ferrer, O. Tribut, et al. "Alzheimer's Disease: The Pharmacological Pathway." *Fundamental and Clinical Pharmacology* 17 (2003): 419–428.

Alzheimer's Disease Education & Referral Center. "Alzheimer's Disease: Unraveling the Mystery." *National Institute on Aging.* Available online at http://www.alzheimers.org/unraveling/07.htm.

Alzheimer's Disease Education & Referral Center. "2003 Progress Report on Alzheimer's Disease." *National Institute on Aging.* Available online at http://www.alzheimers.org.

American Association for Geriatric Psychiatry. "An Interdisciplinary Approach for Improved Patient Outcomes in Dementia." *American Association for Geriatric Psychiatry.* Available online at http://www.cmecorner.com/macmcm/AAGP/aagp2003_01.htm.

American Health Assistance Foundation. "A History of Alzheimer's Disease." *American Health Assistance Foundation.* Available online at http://www.ahaf.org/alzdis/about/adhistory.htm.

Bentué-Ferrer, D., O. Tribut, E. Polard, and H. Allain. "Clinically Significant Drug Interactions With Cholinesterase Inhibitor." *CNS Drugs* 17 (2003): 947–963.

Crismon, M. L., and A. Eggert. "Alzheimer's Disease." In DiPiro, Joseph T., et al. (ed.). *Pharmacotherapy: A Pathophysiologic Approach*, 4th ed. Stamford, CT: Appleton & Lange, 1999.

Cummings, J. L. "Alzheimer's Disease." *New England Journal of Medicine* 351 (2004): 56–67.

Cummings, J. L., J. C. Frank, D. Cherry, et al. "Guidelines for Managing Alzheimer's Disease: Part II Treatment." *American Family Physician* 65 (2002): 2525–2534.

Deutsch, S. I., R. B. Rosse, L. H. Deutsch, and J. Eller. "Pharmacotherapy of Alzheimer's Disease: New Treatments." *Psychiatric Times* (July 2004): 74–79.

Doraiswamy, P. M. "Non-Cholinergic Strategies for Treating and Preventing Alzheimer's Disease." *CNS Drugs* 16 (2002): 811–824.

Farlow, M. R. "NMDA Receptor Antagonists: A New Therapeutic Approach for Alzheimer's Disease." *Geriatrics* 59 (2004): 22–27.

Geldmacher, D. S. "Long-term Cholinesterase Inhibitor Therapy for Alzheimer's Disease: Practical Considerations for the Primary Care Physician." *Primary Care Companion Journal of Clinical Psychiatry* 5 (2003): 251–259.

Geriatric Mental Health Foundation. "Caring for the Alzheimer's Patient." *American Association of Geriatric Physicians.* Available online at http://www.AAGPonline.org.

Hake, A.M. "Treatment of Alzheimer's Disease with Cholinesterase Inhibitors." *Clinical Geriatrics* 10 (2002).

Hill, J. W., R. Futterman, S. Duttagupta, et al. "Alzheimer's Disease and Related Dementias Increase Costs of Comorbidities in Managed Care." *Neurology* 58 (2002): 62–70.

Ibach, B., and E. Haen. "Acetylcholinesterase Inhibition in Alzheimer's Disease." *Current Pharmaceutical Design* 10 (2004): 231–251.

Johannsen, P. "Long-term Cholinesterase Inhibitor Treatment of Alzheimer's Disease." *CNS Drugs* 18 (2004):757–768.

Johnson, J. G. "The Brain & Five Senses." *The World of Biology.* Available online at http://www.srinet.net/~jgjohso/brain.html.

Larson, E. B., M-F. Shadlen, L. Wang, et al. "Early Symptoms Help Predict Survival Time in Patients with Alzheimer's Disease." Summaries for Patients. *Annals of Internal Medicine* (2004).

Levy, M. L. "Cholinergic Therapy for Alzheimer's Disease." *Annals of Long-Term Care* 6 (1998).

Merck & Co., Inc. "Chapter 40: Dementia." *The Merck Manual of Geriatrics.* Available online at http://www.merck.com/mrkshared/mm_geriatrics/sec5/ch40.jsp.

National Center for Chronic Disease Prevention and Health Promotion, Centers for Disease Control and Prevention. "The Growing Problem of Alzheimer's Disease." Special Focus: Healthy Aging. *Chronic Disease Notes & Reports* (1999).

Pietrzik, C., and C. Behl. "Concepts for the Treatment of Alzheimer's Disease: Molecular Mechanisms and Clinical Application." *International Journal of Experimental Pathology* 86 (2005): 173–185.

Shirley, K. L., and M. W. Jann. "Dementia." In PSAP Editorial Board. *Pharmacotherapy Self-Assessment Program—Neurology,* 4th ed. Kansas City, MO: American College of Clinical Pharmacy, 2002, pp. 167–196.

Small, G. W., D. D. McDonnell, R. L. Brooks, and G. Papadopoulos. "The Impact of Symptom Severity on the Cost of Alzheimer's Disease." *Journal of the American Geriatric Society* 50 (2002): 321–327.

TIME: Toolkit of Instruments to Measure End-of-life Care. "Caregiver Well-being." *Center for Gerontology and Healthcare Research (Brown University).* Available online at http://www.chhr.brown.edu/PCOC/familyburden.htm.

Bibliography

Who Named It? "Alois Alzheimer." *Whonamedit.com.* Available online at http://www.whonamedit.com/doctor.cfm/177.html.

Wilkinson, D. G., P. T. Francis, E. Schwann, and J. Payne-Parrish. "Cholinesterase Inhibitors Used in the Treatment of Alzheimer's Disease." *Drugs Aging* 21 (2004): 453–478.

Further Reading

Crismon, M. L., and A. Eggert. "Alzheimer's Disease." In DiPiro, Joseph T., et al. (ed.). *Pharmacotherapy: A Pathophysiologic Approach*, 4th ed. Stamford, CT: Appleton & Lange, 1999.

Cummings, J. L., J. C. Frank, D. Cherry, et al. "Guidelines for Managing Alzheimer's Disease: Part II Treatment." *American Family Physician* 65 (2002): 2525–2534.

Deutsch, S. I., R. B. Rosse, L. H. Deutsch, and J. Eller. "Pharmacotherapy of Alzheimer's Disease: New Treatments." *Psychiatric Times* (July 2004): 74–79.

National Center for Chronic Disease Prevention and Health Promotion, Centers for Disease Control and Prevention. "The Growing Problem of Alzheimer's Disease." Special Focus: Healthy Aging. *Chronic Disease Notes & Reports* (1999).

Shirley, K. L., and M. W. Jann. "Dementia." In PSAP Editorial Board. *Pharmacotherapy Self-Assessment Program—Neurology*, 4th ed. Kansas City, MO: American College of Clinical Pharmacy, 2002, pp. 167–196.

Websites

http://www.alzheimers.about.com.
About Alzheimer's.

http://www.alz.org.
Alzheimer's Association.

http://www.alzheimers.org.
Alzheimer's Disease Education & Referral Center. "Alzheimer's Disease: Unraveling the Mystery." National Institute on Aging.

http://www.caregiving.org.
National Alliance for Caregiving.

http://www.ncoa.org.
National Council on Aging.

http://www.nimh.nih.gov.
National Institute of Mental Health.

http://www.nia.nih.gov.
National Institute on Aging.

Index

Index

Index

Picture Credits

About the Author

Cynthia Borda holds a Bachelor of Pharmacy from the University of Pittsburgh Pharmacy School, a Master of Business Administration in Health Management and Science Administration from Widener University, and a Doctorate of Pharmacy from the University of Colorado. She is a licensed Pharmacist in the state of Pennsylvania. Dr. Borda's career has spanned all aspects of pharmacy from hospital pharmacist, to Director of Pharmacy at Children's Seashore House in Philadelphia, PA, to medical science liaison at Roche Pharmaceuticals. She continues to work as a medical writer and consultant, while also working as a preceptor to Doctorate of Pharmacy candidates in an ambulatory clinic, a clinical pharmacist at a local hospital, and lecturing on various healthcare topics.

Dr. Borda lives in Buck County, PA, with her husband and two children where she volunteers at her children's schools, and on community committees.

About the Editor

David J. Triggle is a University Professor and a Distinguished Professor in the School of Pharmacy and Pharmaceutical Sciences at the State University of New York at Buffalo. He studied in the United Kingdom and earned his B.Sc. degree in Chemistry from the University of Southampton and a Ph.D. degree in Chemistry at the University of Hull. Following post-doctoral work at the University of Ottawa in Canada and the University of London in the United Kingdom, he assumed a position at the School of Pharmacy at Buffalo. He served as Chairman of the Department of Biochemical Pharmacology from 1971 to 1985 and as Dean of the School of Pharmacy from 1985 to 1995. From 1995 to 2001 he served as the Dean of the Graduate School, and as the University Provost from 2000 to 2001. He is the author of several books dealing with the chemical pharmacology of the autonomic nervous system and drug-receptor interactions, some 400 scientific publications, and has delivered over 1,000 lectures worldwide on his research.